the

SECRET

of

FINDING
BIG
WINNERS

in the

STOCK
MARKET

F.R. MARGOLIUS

PROBUS PUBLISHING COMPANY
Chicago, Illinois

Library of Congress Cataloging-in-Publication Data
Margolius, F. R.
    The secret of finding big winners in the stock market / F.R. "Bud" Margolius.
    p. cm.
  ISBN 1-55738-281-6
  1. Stock-exchange. 2. Investments. I. Title.
HG4551.M34 1991
332.63'22—dc20   91-28036

This book is dedicated to the memory of

Ralph S. Margolius
1909 - 1973

Whatever good traits I may possess he taught me—not by
words, but by example.

———————————

"The sophisticated investor works from a predetermined logic
or method. Because of this he or she is prepared for any kind of
market activity. The market, or a stock, may very well go up or
down, but it is what you have already decided to do at these
points that will, in most cases, bring you profits."

Introduction to *The Wall Street Reader*, edited
by Bill Adler. Published by The World
Publishing Company, 1970.

Contents

Foreword   *vii*
Preface   *xi*

1 Introduction   1

Myth No. 1   5
Myth No. 2   5

2 Selection Factors   7

Section A: Increased Earnings   7
   "But" No. 1   8
   "But" No. 2   9
Section B: The Price/Earnings Ratio   11
Section C: Relation of P/E to Growth   12
Section D: The Financial Situation   13
Section E: The Overall Quality   14
Section F: Summary   14

3 Stock Selection and Purchase   15

Section A: Picking the "Semi-Finalists"   16
   Index   16
   Ticker Symbol   16
   Name of Issue   19
   Com. Rank. & Pfd. Rating   19
   Par Value   19
   Inst. Hold.   19
   Principal Business   19

Price Range   19
Month's Sales in 100's   19
Last Sale or Bid   20
% Div. Yield   20
Cash Div. Ea. Yr. Since 20   20
P/E Ratio   20
Dividends   20
Financial Position   20
Capitalization   21
Earnings   21
Interim Earnings   21
Section B: Awarding Points   26
Section C: The Final Selection   33
Section D: Stock Purchases   35
Section E: An Illustration of the System   38
Section F: Summary   39

4 The Ultra-Conservative Investor   45

Purchase Only A+ Rated Stocks   46
Use a Combination System   46

5 Stock Sales and Additional Purchases   49

Section A: Stock Sheet   49
Section B: Summary Sheet   51
Section C: Dividend Record   53
Section D: Weekly Price Chart   53
Section E: Continuing the Illustration   59
Section F: Additional Purchases   69
Section G: Summary   76

6 Conclusion   77

Appendices   79
    Appendix A   79
    Appendix B   83
    Appendix C   85
    Appendix D   93

Index   147

Foreword

The system employed by the author to make a profit by investing in the stock market is a "techno-fundamental" system.

Since techno-fundamental obviously means a combination of technical and fundamental analysis of price movement, let's take a moment to discuss each of these terms.

Section A: Technical Analysis

The stock market technician, or technical analyst, is one who attempts to predict the future price movement of a stock based solely on observation and analysis of the past price history of the stock — or on a combination of price and volume. This analysis is almost always accomplished through the use of various types of price charts.

Technical analysis of stocks has been going on as a serious approach to investment since the turn of the century. There have been innumerable different charts devised, but generally they fall into just two types: bar charts and point-and-figure charts.

Those technicians who use bar charts will frequently base their system of price projections on a combination of past price movement and volume. Figure 1 shows a typical bar chart.

Point-and-figure chartists base their forecasts of future price movement strictly on past prices, completely ignoring both time and volume. Figure 2 shows a typical point-and-figure chart. The chartist records upward price movement with x's and downward movements with o's.

How can these technicians expect to predict what a stock's price will do in the future, based on past price performance? Their argument is that a chart of prices will tend to consolidate into certain discernible patterns. Once these patterns have been formed, the price will sooner or later break out of these patterns. If the break-out is on the upside, the price will continue to rise,

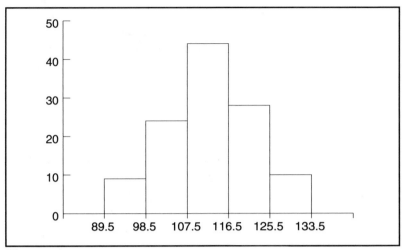

Figure 1

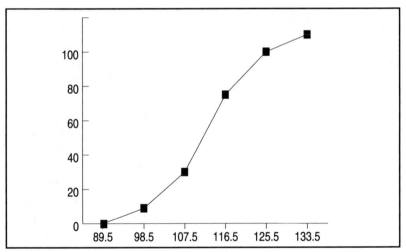

Figure 2

so a buy signal is indicated. Conversely, if the break-out is on the downside, the price can be expected to continue to decline.

The one tool that all competent technicians employ is the use of a stop-loss. They realize that their signals are far from infallible, so their theory is this: accept small losses when the signals prove to be false; ride the signals for large gains when they are correct.

Why do technical analysts ignore every aspect of a company's stock except its price? Their theory is that all factors that cause a stock's price to move up or down or sideways are reflected in the price. Since it is virtually impossible to discover or predict all the good or bad things that can happen — or have happened to a company, don't even attempt such a prodigious feat; let the price tell you!

It's not within the scope of this book to go into detail regarding chart analysis. Neither is it my purpose to argue the merits of technical analysis. Those interested in pursuing the subject will find scores of excellent books available.

Section B: Fundamental Analysis

The fundamentalist will carefully analyze the company in which he is considering investing. What are the prospects for the industry in which the company is engaged? How competent is the management? How sound is the balance sheet? What are the prospects for earnings growth? Are the price-earnings ratio and book value at a historically low figure? And on and on.

Because of the radically different approach of the pure technician as opposed to the pure fundamentalist, the former usually buys for the short term, while the latter tends to invest for the long run.

Section C: Techno-Fundamental Analysis

Perhaps the main weakness of the fundamental approach is that the user tends to "fall in love" with a stock. After a meticulous investigation of the company, the investor finds it to be an excellent investment, so he buys the stock. Downside price movements, he is convinced, have to be temporary for such a great company, so he fails to use a stop-loss, or else decides to lower or cancel his stop-loss if and when the price declines. Many a fortune has been lost on stocks that couldn't fail to appreciate in price — but nevertheless did.

The main weakness of purely technical trading, in my opinion, is the short duration of most trades. This factor causes the investor to have most of his profits taken away in commissions. Moreover, by being stopped out when a price reaction goes a little further than anticipated by his charts, the technician often finds himself left out when a stock climbs to unexpected heights.

Therefore various combinations of the technical and fundamental systems, known as techno-fundamental systems, have gained extreme popularity. Those who employ a techno-fundamental system believe that there are excellent points to be considered by each of the above methods, but also weaknesses that can be eliminated — or at least reduced — by using features of both methods.

That is what the system described in this book attempts to do.

Preface

What "wins" and what doesn't on Wall Street? Clearly, greed, fear, stubbornness and a whole host of emotional reactions do *not* win. Discipline, maturity, insight and, most of all, a "system," *do* win. And that, of course, is what *The Secret of Finding Big Winners in the Stock Market* is all about.

This book is for those who will take the time to learn a simple investment system, one that does not require even a personal computer. A pad and pencil, one basic reference book, any small calculator, patience and a little bit of time are the requirements.

Like every investor, veteran or novice, you want to improve your odds of making sound investment decisions without all the emotional and informational "clutter" that passes as investment advice. Fundamentally, you must seek companies which have a greater than average chance of prospering over time because they have a history of sustained earnings and solid management. The system you are about to learn uses Weighted Average Growth as a means to identify just these kinds of companies. It allows you to rank companies and their performance in such a way as to make your investment decision—both, buy and sell easier and more profitable.

Keep in mind that not every investment decision you make will be the correct one; however, with practice, good information and a little care, you too can improve your odds.

Good luck and happy hunting for those big winners!

Introduction

You know, there are actually hundreds of systems that have been expounded for making money in the stock market. Many systems are so involved that you'd have to have a Ph.D. in math to follow them. Recently I saw a book of this type where I literally was unable to follow the method by the time I reached page two!

Nevertheless I am convinced that, to make money in the market with some degree of consistency, you must follow a system. It amazes me that a person will spend forty to sixty hours a week for years on end to make money in his business; then he'll phone his broker and ask what stock he recommends so he can invest several thousand dollars.

Those other business decisions might put a few hundred dollars in his pocket and are the result of many hours of study and research. Investment decisions affecting many thousands of dollars are made in a matter of minutes by talking to the broker, listening to a friend's "hot tip" or scanning the recommendations of an advisory service.

Speaking of taking the advice of brokers, an article appeared in the Wall Street Journal of November 13, 1990 that showed how the major securities firms fared in picking stocks for the past fifty-one months. See Table 1.1

These are the firms with some of the largest and most prestigious research departments in the world. Yet, the best of them beat the Dow Industrial Average by a nominal percentage—and eight of the ten didn't even manage to do that!

Table 1.1

BROKERAGE HOUSE	
Smith Barney	+ 55.8%
Goldman Sachs	52.6%
Shearson Lehman	51.5%
Merrill Lynch	28.4%
PaineWebber	26.8%
Raymond James	26.3%
Dean Witter	22.0%
A. G. Edwards	21.1%
Kidder Peabody	20.8%
Prudential–Bache	16.7%
* * *	
Dow Jones Industrial Average 51.8% (Increase)	
S & P 500-stock Index 41.0% (Increase)	

The message this conveys is rather obvious: you're not going to get rich in the market by buying and selling when the "experts" advise. After all, even the most successful of them showed a return of just over 13% per year, while the average return of the ten firms was just over 7-1/2% per year.

If you are satisfied with such a return, you'd be better off putting your money in Treasury Notes; they would give you about the same return with little risk.

Not only should you follow a system, but the system should be as mechanical as possible. The reason why this factor is of such vital importance is that it eliminates emotions from your investment decisions. Emotions can be detrimental to sound judgment when making buy or sell decisions in the stock market. What often happens is similar to the following:

- Jack buys a stock at 60 dollars a share, because a friend told him it will surely go up. (GREED)

- A month later the stock is down to 48 dollars, but Jack holds on believing it will surely go up. (PRIDE, STUBBORNNESS)

- Next month it's up to 55. Jack is sure he was right after all. (HOPE)

- The following month the stock drops to 40 dollars a share, so Jack panics and sells at the lowest point the stock will reach. (FEAR)

These emotions affect not only the newcomers in the market, but also the most experienced traders, including professionals. The following quote goes all the way back to the December 12, 1977 issue of *Barron's*:

"...in his December letter to clients..., Harold Erlich raises a long list of pertinent questions. 'What makes so many portfolio managers wary of stocks—*after* prices have declined so much? Why were most of these same people essentially bullish last January, when the Dow Industrials were over 1,000..? (Author's note: at the time this article appeared, the Dow was at 815.) Have business and political prospects darkened enough to justify this newly found pessimism, or has the decline of the market engendered fears that were not present when stock prices were more buoyant? Has it not occurred to these professionals that a drop of 20% for the Dow—and much more for many leading stocks—has compensated for a fair proportion of the bad news that has made headlines for many months?'"

Harold continues, answering his own questions. "To paraphrase the words of the Bard, their difficulty lies not in the stars, not in reality, but in themselves. Emotional problems prevent them from translating intellectual knowledge into practice. To us, the consensus among investment professionals seems so bearish—at least in private—that we have assigned greater odds to the bullish possibilities than we did earlier this year...."

*   *   *   *

As one who's tried to beat the market for close to half a century, I recently paused to ask myself a very basic question: WHY DOES A STOCK GO UP IN PRICE?

The standard answer, of course, is the same one I received several decades ago as a student at the Wharton School of the University of Pennsylvania:

"The stock market is the very essence of capitalism. It's the purest form, the most classic example of supply and demand ever devised by man. When more people want to buy than want to sell, the price of a stock rises. And when there are more sellers than buyers, the price declines."

That's not an actual quote, but it's pretty close to what I was told then—and to what I've been hearing ever since. The only trouble with that explanation is that it fails to tell you WHY more people want to buy, or more people want to sell.

It took me some forty years to find the answer. In case you're a bit impatient and don't want to search that long, I'll tell you now. But first let me say that I'm not talking about a stock rising five or six points before falling back; when you sell out every time you have a small profit, the only person who becomes wealthy is your broker! I'm speaking of dynamic, sustained price gains that continue for long periods of time—because they are the only stocks that can make you rich.

Like all great truths, the answer to why more people want to buy, or more people want to sell is amazingly simple: *stocks go up in price because the company's earnings go up*. Look at this fictitious example:

> In 1980, XYZ earned $1.00 per share; it's price was 8; it's P/E* was 8 times earnings.
> In 1981 it earned $2.00 per share; its price was 16; its P/E was still 8 times earnings.
> In 1982 it earned $3.00 per share; its price was 24; its P/E was still 8 times earnings.
> In 1983 it earned $5.00 per share; its price was 40; its P/E was still 8 times earnings.

So there you have a stock that never really caught the public's eyes. In three years it increased its earnings by 500%, an average of 167% per year, but it was still valued by the investment community at a very conservative eight times earnings. Of course, if the public had spotted this

---

*Price to earnings ratio. This is figured by dividing the current price by the annual earnings per share.

little gem and jumped on it, and pushed its price up to twenty-five times earnings (which frequently happens), XYZ would have been selling in 1983 at 125!

But are there companies in real life like XYZ? You bet there are! I'm going to tell you how to find them.

First we're going to dispel a couple of myths:

Myth No. 1

Big Money Can Only Be Made In Glamour Industry Companies.
Today that might mean you should only buy companies in electronics, aerospace, miracle drugs, etc. This is not true, although you certainly wouldn't rule out companies in these industries. But the fact is it isn't always the industry, but rather the management of the company that has the greater importance. You'll see the truth of this statement as we progress.

Myth No. 2

You'll Do Better In The Long Run If You Stick To The Large, Dependable Corporations. Brokers love this one. They know that if they tell the lady (whose husband just dropped dead and left her a few hundred thousand dollars) to buy IBM or 3M or General Motors, she won't faint with fright. But these are companies that made fortunes for investors forty or fifty years ago. It's time to seek out the new IBMs.

We have a good idea by now of what kind of companies we're searching for. If we can somehow weed through the thousands of publicly traded stocks and come up with a few that best meet the qualifications listed below, we shall be well on our way to successful investment in the stock market.

Our job, then, is to discover the best of the stocks of:
1. Companies with an unbroken record of increased earnings for the past several years.
2. Companies whose fine earnings records have not yet been spotted by the investment community.
3. Companies that show they are soundly managed because, in spite of their rapid, sustained growth, their basic financial situation is still healthy.

Selection Factors 2

We are about to discuss the vital factors that separate the winning stocks from the also-rans. As mentioned in the preceding chapter, earning power is the primary force that fuels a stock in its upward climb, so three of the five factors that we consider are related directly to earnings.

If, however, 100% of our analysis of a stock was based on earnings, we would inevitably run into trouble. This would be analogous to selecting a new automobile based on nothing but how fast it could accelerate from zero to a hundred miles per hour. Little good that would do if the engine burned out in a few months or the body wasn't sturdy enough to support such awesome power.

In addition to earning power, we shall include two factors that measure the financial stability and overall quality of the company. We should thus end up with "autos" that are both fast and sturdy.

Section A: Increased Earnings

Believe it or not, we are going to find so many companies that can boast of three or four or more years of increased earnings, that we have to be even stricter. In order to qualify as a candidate for purchase, the company's average annual increase in earnings must be at least 25%. But that still doesn't satisfy the earnings requirement. For instance, look at the earnings per share (EPS) of these two stocks:

	1984	1985	1986	1987	1988
Company "A"	.01	.09	.25	.35	.39
Company "B"	.01	.06	.10	.18	.39

Both companies have increased their earnings by far more than an average of 25% per year, however, Company A's earnings have increased percentage-wise as follows:

1985: 800% (.09 – .01 = .08; .08 ÷ .01 = 8.00, or 800%)
1986: 178% (.25 – .09 = .16; .16 ÷ .09 = 1.777, or 178%)
1987: 40% (.35 – .25 = .10; .10 ÷ .25 = .40, or 40%)
1988: 11% (.39 – .35 = .04; .04 ÷ .35 = .114, or 11%)

NOTE: The arithmetic involved in figuring percentage increases is quite simple, and very quick by using any small calculator:

1.   Subtract the present year's earnings from the previous year's earnings.
2.   Divide the difference by the previous year's earnings.

Overall, from 1984 earnings of .01 cents per share to 1988 earnings of .39 cents per share, earnings have increased a whopping 3800% (.39 – .01 = .38; .38 ÷ .01 = 38.00, or 3800%). There are, however, some obvious "buts" to making a categorical statement that "Here is a company that has increased earnings per share 3800% in five years and can be expected to continue to do so."

"But" No. 1

The percentage increase is exaggerated because of the earnings of only .01 cent in the first year. For our analysis, *the percentage earnings increase in any one year will be limited to a maximum of 200%.* Recalculating Company A's earnings with the above revision gives us:

1985:	200%	1987:	40%
1986:	178%	1988:	11%

Average increase for four years:
$$200 + 178 + 40 + 11 = 429 \div 4 = 107\%.$$

"But" No. 2

Whereas Company A was flying along with tremendous percentage increases in earnings in 1985 and 1986, it was struggling in the last two years to keep up with its past performance. Earnings increases were down to 40% in 1987 and only 11% in 1988.

Now let's look at Company B. Its percentage increases were:

1985: 200% (Actually $.06 - .01 = .05; .05 \div .01 = 5.00$, or 500%)
1986: 67% ($.10 - .06 = .04; .04 \div .06 = .666$, or 67%)
1987: 80% ($.18 - .10 = .08; .08 \div .10 = .80$, or 80%)
1988: 117% ($.39 - .18 = .21; .21 \div .18 = 1.166$, or 117%)

Average increase for four years:
$$200 + 67 + 80 + 117 = 464 \div 4 = 116\%.$$

Not only was Company B's average increase (figured annually) higher than Company A's, but more important, the recent increases (1987 and 1988) showed a growing momentum. It is certainly logical to assume that Company B's chances of continued earnings growth are far superior to that of Company A. Note: Both companies went from $.01$ to $.39 = 3800\%$.

How can we make a more realistic comparison of these companies? The answer lies in showing, not just the average earnings growth, but a **weighted average growth** placing stronger emphasis on the more recent years. Here's how we do that:

Let's continue to use as examples Companies A and B, whose earnings are repeated in Table 2.1:

Table 2.1

	Earnings Per Share				
	1st yr.	2nd yr.	3rd yr.	4th yr.	5th yr.
	1984	*1985*	*1986*	*1987*	*1988*
Company A	.01	.09	.25	.35	.39
Company B	.01	.06	.10	.18	.39

To figure the Weighted Average Growth (WAG):

1. Figure the growth for the second year vs. the first year (maximum 200%).

2. Figure the growth for the third year vs. the second year and multiply by two (maximum 400%).

3. Figure the growth for the fourth year vs. the third year and multiply by three (maximum 600%).

4. Figure the growth for the fifth year vs. the fourth year and multiply by four (maximum 800%).

5. Add the above results together and divide by ten.

A perfect score would be 200 + 400 + 600 + 800 = 2,000 ÷ 10 = 200, but don't expect to ever see this! Let's see how that works out with our two fictitious companies:

Weighted Average Growth (WAG)
Company A:
2nd yr. (1985) vs. 1st yr. (1984) = 200%
3rd yr. (1986) vs. 2nd yr. (1985) = 178% x 2 = 356%
4th yr. (1987) vs. 3rd yr. (1986) = 40% x 3 = 120%
5th yr. (1988) vs. 4th yr. (1987) = 11% x 4 = 44%
200 + 356 + 120 + 44 = 720 ÷ 10 = 72%
Company B:
2nd yr. (1985) vs. 1st yr. (1984) = 200%
3rd yr. (1986) vs. 2nd yr. (1985) = 67% x 2 = 134%
4th yr. (1987) vs. 3rd yr. (1986) = 80% x 3 = 240%
5th yr. (1988) vs. 4th yr. (1987) = 117% x 4 = 468%
200 + 134 + 240 + 468 = 1042 ÷ 10 = 104.2%

Using an unweighted average increase, Company B's average growth is 116% versus 107% for Company A, or 9% greater. Our more realistic Weighted Average Growth (WAG) shows Company B's growth is 104% versus 72% or 31% greater.

At the beginning of this chapter, it was stated that we are looking for companies with three, four or more years of uninterrupted earnings increases. The examples cited so far concerned companies with four years of increased earnings. We shall now look at an example of a company which has a history of earnings increases for the past three years:

	1984	1985	1986	1987	1988
d.	.20	.18	.40	.65	.90

The WAG would be computed as follows (the .20 cent per share deficit for 1984 is ignored in the computation):

.40 − .18 = .22 ÷ .18 = 122%
.65 − .40 = .25 ÷ .40 = 63% x 2 = 126%
.90 − .65 = .25 ÷ .65 = 38% x 3 = 114%

The three figures are then divided by six, rather than ten:

122 + 128 + 114 = 362 ÷ 6 = 60.3% WAG

For such a company to be eligible as a candidate for purchase, earnings must have doubled in the years since it became profitable—an average earnings increase of 33 1/3% or more.

Section B:
The Price/Earnings Ratio

On April 30, 1990 Ducommon, Inc. (symbol DCO), an American Stock Exchange stock, closed at 3 7/8. On the same day Dow Chemical (symbol DOW on the New York Stock Exchange) closed at 61 3/4. Which stock was cheaper?

On the face of it, DCO was at a lower price. After all, you could buy fifteen shares of this stock for less than you would pay for one share of DOW. Why would anyone buy DOW when DCO (and thousands of other stocks) could be bought for less? How do you know whether a stock's price is high or low?

The answer comes right back to what we just discussed in the preceding section—earnings. DOW at 61 3/4 was selling at a low eight times earnings, while DCO sold at a precarious forty-three times earnings. Whereas Dow Chemical would be a good, conservative investment, you'd better have a mighty good reason for buying Ducommon!

There is only one way to judge whether a stock is selling at a cheap price or an expensive price—and that is its ratio of price to earnings, or its P/E. Only the P/E gives you an idea of whether a stock is under-priced, fairly priced or overpriced. Naturally, a stock such as Company B with its fine growth record would command a higher P/E than a stock whose earnings were flat or erratic.

We shall be looking for stocks which are not overpriced, stocks with relatively low P/E ratios compared to the overall P/E ratio of the market as measured by the Dow Jones Industrial Average or the S & P 500.

Section C:
Relation of P/E to Growth

The P/E ratio shows if the stock has been fairly priced by the investment community. The P/E alone will not show how much the price reflects the chances of a stock to increase earnings, based on its history of growth. Consider two more fictitious stocks:

	1984	1985	1986	1987	1988	Current Price	P/E Ratio
Co. C:	.50	.75	.40	.80	.80	8	10
Co. D:	.10	.16	.30	.50	.80	8	10

Both stocks are selling for $8 per share, or ten times earnings. However, whereas Company D shows a history of uninterrupted healthy growth, Company C's earnings are quite erratic. We would not consider a purchase of Company C, but Company D might well turn out to be a likely candidate for purchase.

Let's look at the WAG for the two stocks:

Company C: (1985) .75 − .50 = .25 ÷ .50 = 50%
(1986) .40 − .75 = −.35 = 0 x 2 = 0
(1987) .80 − .40 = .40 ÷ .40 = 100 x 3 = 300%
(1988) .80 − .80 = 0 x 4 = 0

WAG: 50 + 0 + 300 + 0 = 350 ÷ 10 = 35%

Company D: (1985) .16 − .10 = .06 ÷ .10 = 60%
(1986) .30 − .16 = .14 ÷ .16 = .875 x 2 = 175%
(1987) .50 − .30 = .20 ÷ .30 = .667 x 3 = 200%
(1988) .80 − .50 = .30 ÷ .50 = .60 x 4 = 240%

WAG: 60 + 175 + 200 + 240 = 675 ÷ 10 = 67.5%

A method of relating the P/E to the company's growth is to divide the P/E by the WAG. The lower the resulting percentage, the healthier and better priced is the stock.

In the above example, Company C's relation of P/E to WAG would be:

P/E (10) ÷ WAG (35) = .2857, or 29%

For Company D:

P/E (10) ÷ WAG (67.5) = .1481, or 15%

Section D:
The Financial Situation

If you are or have been in a position of financial responsibility with a rapidly growing company, you are painfully aware of the fact that cash flow can be an agonizing problem. Sales are growing fast, maybe 30% or 40% or more per year. This means you have to constantly carry more inventory. You need to add more and more employees, causing the payroll to climb constantly. You rent or build an office, warehouse or plant that you figure will meet your needs for twenty years—and five or six years later the space is outgrown.

Remember in Chapter 1 we said "it isn't the industry that's important, but the management of the company." A company with the managers who know how to manage for growth has the best chance of continuing rapid growth.

This will be reflected in many areas, but the easiest place to spot the efficiency of management is its ability to show a satisfactory ratio of current assets to current liabilities—the most important factor in a healthy balance sheet.

Section E:
The Overall Quality

In the following chapter, we shall discuss the Standard & Poor's Corporation Security Owner's Stock Guide. One of its features is a rating of the investment quality of the stock. An A+ is the top rating—a D is the bottom. Along with the other items covered above, we shall give consideration to the S & P ratings when choosing the stocks to buy.

Section F: Summary

The following factors will be considered in our choice of candidates of stocks to purchase:

1. Growth, as measured by the WAG.

2. Value, as measured by:

    a. The P/E ratio.

    b. The relation of the P/E ratio to growth.

3. Stability, as measured by the company's balance sheet.

4. Overall quality, as measured by the S & P rating.

In the following chapter, you will discover that only about 5% of the listed stocks will qualify to be considered as candidates for purchase—and by the time we are ready to make our final choice, only 1% will be considered.

Nothing is a sure thing in the stock market, but when you're choosing which stocks to buy from the top 1%, the odds are more favorable!

Stock Selection and Purchase 3

We are now ready to begin looking for our candidates for purchase. There's bad news and good news; fortunately the items of good news outnumber the bad news four to one.

First the bad news:

To set up the system, you're going to have to put in as much as twenty or thirty hours of work.

Now the good news:

1. You won't have to put this much time into our system again for a very long time, perhaps several years.

2. While the work mentioned in the bad news is time consuming, you will find it to be rather simple once you read the explanation and actually begin.

3. Once the work of selecting and buying stocks is completed, you'll need to spend less than an hour a week maintaining the system.

4. The only research tool you'll need is a wonderfully compact booklet called, appropriately enough, "Stock Guide." This little gem is published monthly by Standard & Poor's Corporation. It costs about $90 per year (twelve monthly issues) and it's well worth it. You may order it from Standard & Poor's Corporation, 25 Broadway, P.O. Box 992, New York, NY 10275-0123.

I would suggest that you obtain a copy of the Stock Guide immediately (it doesn't have to be the current copy), either by asking your broker if he has an extra copy, or if you don't yet have a broker, phone Standard & Poor's at (212) 208-8769.

Section A:
Picking the "Semi-Finalists"

The Statistical Section of the Stock Guide is what we are interested in. It's about 240 pages in length. Each page has about forty-five numbered lines, representing that number of stocks, listed alphabetically. Figure 3.1 is a sample page, so you may follow the procedure outlined below.

A brief explanation of the components of this section follows, reading from left to right (see Figure 3.1):

Index

The index numbers are a visual guide to the data that follows; see last paragraph, page 23.

Ticker Symbol

Since these symbols will be used frequently, and are used by your broker to enter in his computer and obtain price and other information on the stock, be very sure to record them accurately.

Generally speaking, stocks traded on the New York and American Stock Exchanges will have one, two or three-letter symbols. Over-the-counter stocks will have NASDAQ Trading System symbols — usually four-letter symbols (if five letters, the last letter will probably be an "A" or "B", meaning a Class A or Class B issue).

Figure 3.1

74 DYA-EDW

Standard & Poor's Corporation

S&P 500 •Options Index	Ticker Symbol	Name of Issue (Call Price of Pfd. Stocks)	Market	Com. Rank. & Pfd. Rating	Par Val.	Inst. Hold Cos.	Inst. Hold Shs. (000)	Principal Business	Price Range 1971-87 High	1971-87 Low	1988 High	1988 Low	1989 High	1989 Low	May Sales in 100s	May, 1989 Last Sale Or Bid High	Low	Last	%Div. Yield	P-E Ratio
1	DYAN	Dyansen Corp	OTC	NR	1¢	10	840	Mkts fine art & related prod	3	⅞	3¼	1 7/16	3½	1 11/16	19909	3½	2⅞	3S		2
2	DYTR	Dyatron Corp	OTC	B−	66⅔¢	16	580	Auto dealer computer serv	15¼	1½	15¼	10¾	16	12¾	2248	16	14½	15¾E		[illegible]
3	DYCO	Dycom Indus	OTC	NR	33⅓¢	31	1120	Telecommunication svcs	16	½	21	9¼	25	15½	9953	18½	15½	15⅝E		[illegible]
4	DYA	Dynamics Corp Amer	NY,M	B+	10¢	32	2402	Appliances,metal fab,power	33¼	¼	23½	16½	24⅞	22¾	634	24⅞	24	24⅞	[illegible]	
5	DRCO	Dynamics Research	OTC,B	B−	10¢	21	1437	Mfr encoders: computer svs	11¼	1/16	11	6½	9	6½	1216	7¾	6⅞	7¼E		9
6	DYNA	Dynascan Corp	OTC	B	33⅓¢	33	2672	Consumer & ind'l electronics	23½	⅞	9⅞	6	11¼	8¾	4853	11⅛	10⅛	11⅛E		[illegible]
7	DYTC	Dynatech Corp	OTC	B−	20¢	96	6285	Communic&med'l pr,sci instr	43½	1/16	24	16½	19¼	17½	6465	18	17½	17¾E		12
•8	ESY	E-Systems	NY,B,M,P,Ph	A	1	192	14560	Electronic sys & ed-defense	44¾	11/16	33½	25½	31⅞	27¼	13537	31⅞	29⅝	30⅞		[illegible]
9	EBMI	E & B Marine Inc	OTC,B	C	1¢	8	79	Dstr of marine supplies	25	5½	6½	2	4	1⅞	3845	4	2 9/16	3⅝E		d
10	EZEM	E-Z-EM Inc	OTC	B−	10¢	29	1519	Mfr diagnostic imag'g prod	18⅞	5⅝	14¾	9¼	14	12	1962	13½	12½	12½E		13
11	EACO	EA Engr Science,Tech	OTC	NR	1¢	9	542	Environmental consult'g svcs	10½	3½	7	4⅞	7½	5¾	624	7½	6¾	7¼E		20
12	EAC	EAC Indus	AS	C	10¢	6	148	Mfrd housing,hardware	17⅞	5/16	8⅝	4⅞	8¼	5½	504	7	5½	6		d
13	EGL	Eagle Clothes	AS	C	1	14	1236	Mfrs menswear:retail svcs	16¾	¼	1⅛	5/16	1⅛	⅞	1553	⅞	⅝	⅝		d
14	EAG	Eagle Financial	AS	NR	1¢	11	541	Savings&loan,Connecticut	14½	7⅞	11¼	7¾	10½	8½	924	10	9½	9¾	[illegible]	10
15	EPI	Eagle-Picher Indus	NY,C,M	C	1¼	96	5245	Ind'l pr: mchy&auto parts	53	5⅞	33¼	12⅝	17½	12⅝	12181	14¾	12⅝	14½		3
16	EGLA	Eagle Telephonics	OTC	NR	1¢	7	395	Mfr telephone keysets/eqp	5¾	½	1⅞	5/16	7/16	¼	1551	⅞	¼	¼		d
17	ETCO	Earth Technology	OTC	NR	10¢	13	448	Enviro/tech consult'g svcs	9⅝	2⅝	5⅝	3¼	6¼	4½	2396	5¼	4½	4⅝	...	12
18	TOOL	Easco Hand Tools	OTC	NR	1¢	36	3067	Mfrs specialized hand tools	13	5¾	13½	6¾	9¼	7½	8446	9¼	7½	9E	...	12
19	ESTD	Eastco Industrial Safety	OTC	B−	1¢	2	48	Mfr protective cloth'g/equip	2 7/16	1/16	6⅞	¾	8¼	5½	8688	8¼	6¼	7⅛E	...	15
20	EALPrD	Eastern Air 11.36%Dep Pfd	AS	NR	1	19	2157	Subsid of Texas Air	23⅞	12¼	18	12⅛	17½	13½	1794	16	15	15¼	...	...
21	Pr E	$2.72cm Pfd (25)	AS	NR	1	1	5		23½	6½	15	7	11¼	5	873	9⅝	8⅞	8⅞	...	...
22	Pr F	$3.24cm Pfd (21.625)	AS	NR	1	11	1573		26¼	6½	15¾	6½	11¾	6⅞	2378	10⅝	9⅝	9¾	...	...
23	Pr G	$3.12cm Jr Pfd(25)	AS	NR	1	2	421		22½	7¼	16½	6¾	11	5⅞	493	10¼	8⅞	9½	...	...
24	EML	Eastern Co	AS,M	B	5	18	598	Mine roof supports:metal fab	18⅝	3⅞	19¼	12¼	15½	13	94	14½	13⅞	13⅞	4.2	13
•25	EFU	Eastern Enterprises	NY,B,C,M,P,Ph	B−	1	130	15907	Coal, river barg'g, Boston Gas	33¼	5½	26¾	21¾	31¼	22¾	31151	31¼	27¾	31	4.5	12
26	EESI	East'n Environmental Svc	OTC	NR	1¢	7	157	Asbestos removal/abatement	12¼	4⅞	6⅞	3	5½	3⅞	4122	4⅞	3⅞	3⅝B	...	13
27	EUA	Eastern Util Assoc	NY,B,M,P	A−	5	96	7091	Util hldg co: Mass & RI elec	40½	8	33½	21½	36½	30⅝	4229	36½	33¼	35⅞	7.0	10
28	EGP	EastGroup Properties SBI	AS	NR	1	16	612	Real estate investment trust	40	3⅞	25¼	20¼	24⅝	21⅞	1094	24½	22	24	10.8	4
•29	EK	Eastman Kodak	NY,B,C,M,P,Ph	A−	2½	950	167509	Photograph apparatus,chem	71	18¼	53¼	39½	49¼	42¼	362128	47⅞	42¼	44¾	4.5	10
30	KDU	East Kodak,Americus(Unit)	AS,M	NR	No	4	1107	Unit Trust For Eastman Kodak	104½	71¼	78½	60¼	73½	64½	508	70	64½	67½E	4.4	...
31	KDS	Score	AS,M	NR	No	5	336	Capital appreciation	46⅝	14½	19	6½	11⅞	5½	5917	11⅞	7⅞	11¼	...	...
32	KDP	Prime	AS,M	NR	No	20	746	divd income pay'g component	67	50½	64⅞	48	64¼	56¾	2033	62¼	56¾	58⅝	5.1	...
•33	ETN	Eaton Corp	NY,B,M,P,Ph	B	50¢	307	22337	Electronic/electric sys,eqp	71⅞	8	57⅝	44⅞	62⅝	54¾	24463	62⅝	57½	61⅛	3.2	10
34	EAVN	Eaton Vance	OTC,B	A	12½¢	27	565	Advisor to mutual funds,cst	32¾	1/16	23½	15	27¾	22	320	24½	23	24	1.7	8
35	ECC	ECC International	NY,M	B+	10¢	33	2442	Computer-contr simulators	14⅝	1/16	8⅞	5¼	7⅞	5⅞	1734	7	6¼	6¾	3.0	75
•36	ECH	Echlin Inc	NY,B,M,P	A	1	207	42949	Auto elec. brak'g sys: replace	25⅞	3¾	18¾	14	18⅞	15½	30671	18⅞	16½	17⅝	4.0	15
•37	ECO	Echo Bay Mines Ltd	AS,B,M,P,Mo,To	B	No	213	23221	Mining:gold & silver	30½	3½	24	13	16⅝	12¾	53122	14	12¾	13⅞	+0.4	23
38	ECILF	ECI Telecom Ltd	OTC	NR	[illegible]	1	33	Electronic telecommun sys	17¼	1⅞	5½	2¼	9¼	4½	6221	9¼	7	8⅛B	...	14
39	EECN	Ecogen Inc	OTC	NR	1¢	20	1405	Dvlps biological pesticides	9¾	3⅝	9	3⅞	5	3¼	2993	4	3¼	4B	...	d
•40	ECL	Ecolab Inc	NY,M,Ph	A−	1	143	19681	Cleaning&sanitizing, chemlawn	33¾	6	27¾	21¼	29⅝	25½	29417	29¼	27	27⅞	2.4	14
41	EEI	Ecology/Environment'A'	AS	NR	1¢	12	299	Evironm'l consult g/test'g	29⅞	8½	14⅞	10⅞	13⅝	9⅛	548	10¾	9½	9⅞	1.2	15
42	EDGC	Edgcomb Corp	OTC	NR	1½	9	1669	Operates metals svc ctrs	6½	1⅛	8⅝	2¼	7⅞	5½	11011	7⅞	6½	7¼B	...	60
43	EBS	Edison Bros Stores	NY,M	B	1	76	4515	Women's shoe store chain	46¾	5⅝	34½	24⅞	49⅞	32	4243	49⅞	45½	49⅞	3.6	14
44	EDO	EDO Corp	NY,B,M	B+	1	31	2147	Electr eq:military,marine	23	1/16	18⅞	10⅝	11⅞	9¾	732	10⅝	9⅞	10	2.8	14
45	ESPC	Education Sys & Pub	OTC	C	1¢	1	17	Commercial printing	5	¼	2¾	½	1	1/16	117	1	¾	1S	...	d
•46	AGE	Edwards(AG)Inc	NY,B,M,P	B−	1	76	8202	Security broker: inv banker	36⅞	⅞	21⅞	15⅞	23¾	18¾	8196	23¾	20	23⅞	2.9	14

Uniform Footnote Explanations-See Page 1. Other: [1]P:Cycle 2. [2]Ph:Cycle 1. [3]CBOE:Cycle 1. [4]P:Cycle 3. [5]P,Vc:Cycle 1. [6]Vc [7]CBOE:Cycle 2. [51]Excl 2M Cl'B'(Cv at 100 to 1). [52]$0.65,'87. [53]Cm:Div in cash or Dep Pfc thru'90,then cash. [54]Dep for1/100 shr of 11.36% Jr Pfd:callable $25. [55]Divd in cash or $2.72Pfc thru'90,then cash. [56]0.0375 Pfc shrs. [57]0.075 Pfc shrs. [58]Divd in cash or $3.24Pfc stk thru'90,then cash. [59]Incl 0.075 Pfd shrs. [60]Divd in cash or $3.24 Pfc stk thru'90,then cash. [61]Divd in cash or $3.12Pfc stk thru'90,then cash. [62]Formerly East'n Gas & Fuel. [63]Subsid Pfd in MS. [64]Fiscal Nov'87 & prior. [65]Represents 1.5 Eastman Kodak com shrs. [66]$4.67,'87. [67]Non-vtg. [68]Ord par 2.40 shekel. [69]Fiscal Jun,'86 & prior,12 Mo Dec,'86 $1.67. [70]$1.60,'88. [71]Investor Gr offer $8 to Jun 16

Source: "Standard & Poor's Stock Guide"

Figure 3.1 ***continued***

DYA-EDW 75

Dividends: Latest Payment: Period $	Date	Ex Div.	Total $: So Far 1989	Ind. Rate	Paid 1988	Financial Position Mil-$: Cash & Equiv.	Curr. Assets	Curr. Liab.	Balance Sheet Date	Capitalization: Lg Trm Debt Mil-$	Shs. 000: Pfd	Com.	Earnings $ Per Shr.: Years End	1985	1986	1987	1988	1989	Last 12 Mos.	Interim Earnings: Period	$ per Shr.: 1988	1989	Index
None Since Public			...	Nil	....	0.13	12.2	8.27	9-30-88	3.10	...	5291	Dc	0.09	0.15	△0.24	P□0.07	....	0.13	3 Mo Mar	d0.01	0.05	1
0.06	4-17-81	3-16		Nil	....	0.43	12.7	5.75	12-31-88	2.10	300	2878	Dc	0.12	0.40	1.11	1.44	....	1.47	3 Mo Mar	0.24	0.27	2
5%Stk	12-21-87	12-1		Nil	....	4.64	34.7	20.2	10-31-88	3.36		4575	Jl	0.30	0.53	0.71	1.01	....	1.25	9 Mo Apr	0.70	0.95	3
S0.10	3-1-89	2-7	0.10	0.20	0.20	25.9	67.4	36.4	12-31-88	18.9	...	4042	Dc	3.66	△0.11	0.89	1.24	....	0.08	3 Mo Mar	1.18	0.02	4
s0.012	4-13-84	3-26		Nil		0.27	36.0	20.5	12-31-88	....	...	5044	Dc	0.03	0.49	0.74	0.81		0.79	12 Wk Mar	0.14	0.12	5
3%Stk	6-1-64	5-6		Nil	....	3.50	93.6	25.4	9-30-88	34.7	...	6730	Dc	0.02	0.85	1.13	P1.04	....	1.05	3 Mo Mar	0.13	0.14	6
None Since Public				Nil	....	22.6	187	52.4	12-31-88	35.7	...	12400	Mr	1.95	2.10	2.08	P1.53	....	1.53				7
Q0.12½	4-5-89	3-13	0.25	0.50	0.50	12.2	500	139	3-31-89	85.0	...	30906	Dc	1.47	2.00	1.95	2.40	E2.80	2.51	3 Mo Mar	0.50	0.61	8
None Since Public				Nil	....	1.29	26.1	23.4	7-03-88	15.8	...	1993	Dc	0.63	d0.64	d2.47	Pd7.39	....	d6.65	3 Mo Mar	d0.84	△d0.10	9
None Since Public				Nil		21.0	44.5	7.86	12-03-88	....		7981	My	0.70	0.87	0.67	0.86		0.96	9 Mo Feb	0.60	0.70	10
None Since Public				Nil	....	3.19	16.6	10.8	11-30-88	0.22	...	2450	Au	0.07	0.53	0.23	0.34	....	0.36	6 Mo Feb	0.16	0.18	11
0.10	12-15-86	11-7		Nil	....	1.26	24.4	9.56	10-31-88	14.5	...	1947	Ja	0.03	d0.50	d1.05	Pd0.85	....	d0.85				12
0.03	9-30-70	9-15		Nil	....	0.44	43.1	24.4	10-29-88	5.09	...	p9214	Jl	0.08	d0.27	0.04	△d0.75		d0.68	6 Mo Jan	d0.03	△0.04	13
Q0.12½	6-1-89	5-9	0.25	0.50	0.37½	Book Value $16.79			12-31-88	25.0	...	2589	Sp				0.58		0.94	6 Mo Mar	0.43	0.69	14
0.28	9-9-88	8-15		Nil	0.84	15.7	338	277	11-30-88	94.3	...	10679	Nv	d12.52	3.80	3.70	d43.54	E5.50	d41.93	3 Mo Feb	0.97	▲2.58	15
None Since Public			...	Nil	....	0.72	16.9	13.6	10-31-88	0.17	...	15244	Dc	d0.34	0.08	0.09	d0.29	....	d0.31	3 Mo Jan	d0.02	d0.04	16
None Since Public			...	Nil	....	4.37	15.4	5.73	11-25-88	0.48	...	2856	Au	0.11	0.31	0.52	0.41	....	0.38	6 Mo Feb	0.18	0.15	17
None Since Public			...	Nil	....	69.0	154	33.6	10-01-88	103	...	13392	Dc	...	...	p0.70	P0.79	....	0.76	3 Mo Mar	0.17	0.14	18
None Paid				Nil	....	0.05	13.2	10.4	12-31-88	0.25	...	2455	Je	Nil	Nil	0.02	0.26	....	0.54	9 Mo Mar	0.10	0.35	19
0.71	5-31-89	5-11	1.42	...	2.84	File Bankruptcy Chapt 11				2296	11026	72519		...	...	b0.31	...	...	....	SF fr Nv'92 thru'97,$25			20
....	5-15-89	5-11		....	1.36	....	...	...		....	2153	...		...	...	b0.31	....	....	....	SF 4% fr Nov'90-'94,$25			21
....	5-15-89	5-11		....	1.62	....	...	...		....	4820	...		...	...	b0.31	....	....	....	SF3%fr Nov'90-99,$21.625			22
....	5-15-89	5-11		....	1.56	....	...	...		....	2153	...		...	...	b0.31	....	....	....	SF 3% fr Nov'90-'99,$25			23
Q0.14	6-15-89	5-15	0.28	0.56	0.54½	1.80	23.6	8.39	10-01-88	5.23	...	1857	Dc	1.18	0.88	1.46	P1.38	....	1.07	3 Mo Mar	0.53	0.22	24
Q0.35	7-3-89	5-31	1.02½	1.40	1.30	112	317	146	12-31-88	264	...	23166	Dc	d1.61	0.82	2.05	2.18	E2.60	2.41	3 Mo Mar	1.12	1.35	25
None Since Public			...	Nil	....	2.65	6.15	1.21	12-31-88	0.42	...	4260	Je	0.01	0.12	0.34	△0.36	....	0.27	6 Mo Dec△	△0.25	0.16	26
Q0.62½	5-15-89	4-25	1.22½	2.50	2.37½	25.1	102	123	9-30-88	534	50	13276	Dc	2.67	2.82	3.46	P2.85	E△3.50	2.94	12 Mo Mar	3.21	2.94	27
Q0.65	4-15-89	4-3	1.30	2.60	2.60	Equity per shr $19.75			9-30-88	17.2	...	2538	Dc	4.40	3.10	2.51	P3.48	....	5.42	3 Mo Mar	0.84	2.78	28
Q0.50	7-3-89	5-25	1.50	2.00	1.85	1075	8684	5850	12-25-88	8129	...	324414	Dc	■0.97	■1.10	3.52	4.31	E4.35	4.13	3 Mo Mar	0.80	0.62	29
Q0.73¾	7-13-89	5-25	2.213	2.95	2.72½	Net Asset Val $73.50			12-31-87	....	...	2252	Dc	...	...	673.50	...	...	....	Expires 4-15-92			30
None Since Public			...	Nil	....	....	...	...		....	...	...	Dc	...	...	...	....	....	....				31
Q0.73¾	7-13-89	5-25	2.213	2.95	2.72½	Termination claim $92				....	...	...	Dc	...	...	...	....	....	....				32
Q0.50	5-25-89	5-2	1.00	2.00	1.666	192	1305	827	12-31-88	655	...	37083	Dc	4.67	2.86	4.77	□6.17	E6.25	6.37	3 Mo Mar	1.61	1.81	33
Q0.10	5-15-89	4-24	0.20	0.40	0.37	10.9	13.2	7.44	10-31-88	14.2	...	3690	Oc	1.27	1.62	2.70	2.74	....	2.64	3 Mo Jan	0.59	0.69	34
Q0.05	7-21-89	6-19	0.15	0.20	0.16	2.45	36.8	12.0	12-31-88	17.3	...	5727	Je	0.50	0.46	0.63	△0.77	....	0.09	9 Mo Mar	△0.56	d0.12	35
Q0.17½	4-18-89	3-31	0.33	0.70	0.60½	8.62	659	238	11-30-88	193	...	55695	Au	1.10	1.11	0.88	1.12	E1.20	1.17	6 Mo Feb	0.45	0.50	36
S0.03½	6-30-89	6-9	0.03½	0.07	0.07	11.0	72.1	71.5	12-31-88	194	...	98874	Dc	0.19	0.30	0.52	0.56	E0.60	0.56	3 Mo Mar	0.11	0.11	37
None Since Public				Nil	....	2.63	31.7	18.8	12-31-87	5.05	...	5041	Dc	d0.69	d1.59	0.17	P0.52	....	0.61	3 Mo Mar	0.10	0.19	38
None Since Public				Nil	....	11.0	11.5	1.53	12-31-88	1.00	...	6681	Dc	pd0.25	pd0.16	pd0.83	d0.52	....	d0.69	3 Mo Mar	d0.10	d0.27	39
Q0.16½	7-14-89	5-14	0.49½	0.66	0.63	18.9	286	229	12-31-88	254	...	27355	Dc	1.45	1.62	▲5.30	1.63	E2.00	1.54	3 Mo Mar	d0.19	d0.28	40
S0.06	6-22-89	5-19	0.12	0.12	0.10	0.11	25.1	9.66	10-29-88	0.93	...	3935	Jl	0.23	0.50	0.64	0.74	E0.65	0.67	6 Mo Jan	0.40	0.33	41
None Since Public			...	Nil	....	3.82	172	101	9-30-88	189	184	8190	Dc		□d0.21	△0.08	P0.24	....	0.13	3 Mo Mar	0.27	0.16	42
Q0.45	6-9-89	5-22	1.35	1.80	1.80	21.9	264	152	10-01-88	102	...	10017	Dc	2.66	3.36	△d2.11	P3.64	....	3.64				43
Q0.07	6-30-89	6-5	0.21	0.28	0.28	32.8	104	49.1	12-31-88	56.5	90	5456	Dc	1.01	0.84	1.01	△0.70	....	0.69	3 Mo Mar	△0.20	0.19	44
None Paid			...	Nil	....	0.13	1.06	0.53	12-31-88	0.08	...	664	Dc	0.34	0.27	d0.05	d0.86	....	d0.86				45
Q0.17	7-1-89	6-5	0.51	0.68	0.68	Equity per shr $14.16			11-30-88	....	...	20562	Fb	1.85	2.59	1.73	P1.70	....	1.70				46

Splits & Divs By Line Reference Index 2-for-1,'86;Adj to 5%,'87. 5-for-4,'86, twice,'87. 3-for-2,'87. 3-for-2,'86. 3-for-1,'88. 2-for-1,'88. 3-for-2,'85,'87. 3-for-2,'85. 2-for-1,'86. ,'86. 2-for-1,'85. 2-for-1,'87. 2-for-1,'86. 3-for-2,'86.

Name of Issue

The precise corporate title is often shortened because of space limitations. Unless otherwise designated, the issue is a common stock. The markets on which the issues are traded are shown; our interest is only in NY (New York Stock Exchange), AS (American Stock Exchange) or OTC (Over-the-Counter) stocks.

Com. Rank. & Pfd. Rating

Since only common stocks are being considered in our system, ignore "Pfd. Rating." The ranking of the common stocks is covered on page 30, paragraph 5.

Par Value

This factor has no relevance to our system.

Inst. Hold.

This factor has no relevance to our system.

Principal Business

The explanation of how to use this section is covered later on in the text. The Stock Guide lists the principal business of the company, i.e., the business (where there are two or more industries in which the company is engaged) from which it derives the greatest proportion of its revenue.

Price Range

This factor has no relevance to our system.

Month's Sales in 100s

This factor has no relevance to our system.

Last Sale or Bid

These are the last sales of the preceding month for New York Stock Exchange and American Stock Exchange issues. For over-the-counter stocks, it is the bid price. If you haven't previously traded OTC stocks, a word of explanation is due.

Every over-the-counter stock has two prices:
1. The price at which the owner of the stock is willing to sell his stock. This is the Asked Price.
2   The price that a buyer is willing to pay. This is the Bid Price.

Thus, if a potential buyer offers $15 per share and the potential seller (owner) demands $16 per share, the price would be 15 bid, 16 asked. If the buyer and seller consumate the deal, it would be at not less than $15 or more than $16.

% Div. Yield

This is figured by dividing the total indicated dividend rate by the stock price per share.

P/E Ratio

We have already discussed this very important factor.

Cash Div. Ea. Yr. Since

This factor has no relevance to our system.

Dividends

In our system, we are only interested in the "% Div. Yield" column.

Financial Position

We are interested in these columns:
"Curr. Assets": This includes cash and equivalents.

"Curr. Liab.": Short term obligations, usually payable on demand, or in not more than twelve months.

The above figures are shown in millions of dollars. E.g., 20 = $20,000,000; 8.62 = $8,620,000; 0.71 = $710,000.

Where no figure is given, see "NOTE" on page 22, paragraph 3.

Capitalization

Our only interest in this section is in the ratio of preferred shares to common shares. Preferred shares receive preference in payment of dividends; should a company get in financial difficulties, preferred shareholders are the first to be paid off. Therefore, companies with a large number of preferred shares outstanding in proportion to the common shares, are not a desirable investment for our system.

Earnings

As you have already learned, this section is vital to our system. The "Last 12 Mos." column indicates earnings computed through the period shown in the Interim Earnings column.

Interim Earnings

The 6-month and 9-month earnings are used in our selection process. The 3-month earnings figures are ignored, since temporary or seasonal factors could make these figures meaningless.

Here's what we are going to do:

1. Beginning with the first page of the Stock Section, check the "Name of Issue." If the issue is a preferred stock, unit trust, or any other issue other than a common stock, proceed to the next line. If it's a foreign stock that pays in American Depository Receipts, proceed to the next line

(you can quickly spot them, as they will have ADR after the company's name).

2. Continue over to the last column on the left hand side of the page, the "P-E ratio." The stock does not qualify for selection if:

    a. This column is blank.

    b. A letter "d" appears in the column.

    c. The figure is higher than twice the current average P/E ratio of the Dow Jones Industrial Average. This average P/E ratio can be obtained in financial newspapers such as *Barron's* or *Investor's Daily*.

3. Continuing from left to right, the next section to observe is the "Financial Position." If "Curr. Assets" do not exceed "Curr. Liab." by 25%, the stock does not qualify.

Note: Certain stocks, such as banks and other financial-type institutions, will show an "Equity Per Share," "Book Value" or "Net Asset Value" in the "Financial Position" section. In such cases, disregard the current assets to current liabilities factor. Eliminate the stock only if it shows a negative equity per share.

4. Now check the following section, "Capitalization." If the stock has preferred stock outstanding, the number of shares of preferred stock must not exceed 10% of the number of common shares. If it does exceed 10%, eliminate that stock from consideration.

5. Next we shall check the "Earnings $ per shr" columns of all stocks that show their earnings for either four or five years; if earnings figures are shown for less than four years, proceed to the next stock. Recall our discussion of increased earnings in Section A of Chapter 2. It was pointed out that we are looking for stocks whose earnings have increased each year and at least doubled from year 1 to year 5 or, if there was a deficit in year 1, earnings that have doubled from year 2 to year 5. Since earnings is

our most important factor in selecting which stocks to purchase, some examples are given below. Where figures appear in both "1989" and "Last 12 mos.," use the 1989 figure. If there is no figure shown for 1989, use the "Last 12 mos" column.

Before proceeding with examples, a word of caution. You will notice an "Index" column on the left side of the left page, the left side of the right page and the right side of the right page. Unless you carefully refer to these line numbers, it's very easy to make an error.

Now we shall proceed to the examples:

1985	1986	1987	1988	1989	Last 12 mos.
.30	.32	.40	.56	.58	

Does not qualify, since earnings would have to be at least .60 cents in 1989 to have doubled.

1985	1986	1987	1988	1989	Last 12 mos.
1.20	1.60	2.50	2.50		3.07

Does not qualify, since earnings did not show an increase in 1988 over 1987.

1985	1986	1987	1988	1989	Last 12 mos.
d .22	.03	.09	.15		.25

Qualifies, since earnings increased each year and doubled in the past four years.

1985	1986	1987	1988	1989	Last 12 mos.
.80	1.80	1.60	3.19	3.40	3.30

Does not qualify since earnings decreased in 1987 vs. 1986.

6. Finally, check the extreme right section, "Interim Earnings." If this section is blank, or if the 3-month EPS (Earnings Per Share) is shown, ignore this section. If a stock's six-month or nine-month EPS shows a decrease, proceed to the next line in the Stock Guide.

If a stock qualifies as a candidate for purchase by all the above factors, put a dash next to it. Use a pencil for this purpose, as ink has a tendency to bleed through the page.

Now turn back to the sample page from the Stock Guide. Of the forty-six stocks listed on this page, you would put a dash beside four of them that qualify. Before reading on, see if you can find them.

The four qualifying stocks are: Line 3 (Dycom Industries); Line 25 (Eastern Enterprises); Line 29 (Eastman Kodak); and Line 34 (Eaton Vance).

Make sure you know why these four qualify and why none of the others do. Table 3.1 shows the factors that keep the others from qualifying.

In the above examples, all the reasons for disqualification at this time are noted. When working on this phase, as soon as the stock fails to qualify, immediately proceed to the next line.

Occasionally you will come upon an unusual entry in the Stock Guide, not covered in this book. You don't know whether to include it as a qualifying stock. What do you do?

My advice is to disqualify it. You will end up with more than enough excellent candidates for purchase without including doubtful selections.

Now you need a very wide sheet of paper to list the stocks you have marked. I use a "data pad" 11" long by 17" wide, which is available at most office supply stores. There are 50 sheets to a pad. You will need these columns:

SYMBOL
NAME OF STOCK
S & P RATING
EXCHANGE
INDUSTRY (Use a number as shown in Appendix A)
P/E
YIELD (If none, put a zero in this column)
END F/Y (the month in which the company's fiscal year ends)
5 columns for Earnings Per Share (EPS)
WAG YR 2 (If Yr. 1 was a deficit, put a dash in this column)
WAG YR 3
WAG YR 4

Table 3.1

Line	Symbol	Sections that Currently Disqualify Stocks
1	DYAN	Earnings $ per share
2	DYTR	Capitalization (too many preferred shares)
4	DYA	P-E Ratio; Earnings $ per share
5	DRCO	Earnings $ per share (last 12 mos. column)
6	DYNA	Earnings $ per share
7	DYTC	Earnings $ per share
8	ESY	Earnings $ per share
9	EMBI	P-E Ratio; Financial Position; Earnings $ per share
10	EZEM	Earnings $ per share
11	EACO	Earnings $ per share
12	EAC	P-E Ratio; Earnings $ per share
13	EGL	P-E Ratio; Earnings $ per share
14	EAG	Earnings $ per share (insufficient data)
15	EPI	Earnings $ per share
16	EGLA	P-E Ratio; Financial Position; Earnings $ per share
17	ETCO	Earnings $ per share; Interim Earnings
18	TOOL	Earnings $ per share
19	ESTO	Earnings $ per share
20/21/ 22/23		Name of Issue (these are all preferred stocks)
24	EML	Earnings $ per share
26	EESI	Earnings $ per share
27	EUA	Financial Position; Earnings $ per share; Interim Earnings
28	EGP	Earnings $ per share
30/31/ 32		Name of Issue (these are unit trusts rather than common stocks)
33	ETN	Earnings $ per share
35	ECC	P-E Ratio; Earnings $ per share; Interim Earnings
36	ECH	Earnings $ per share
37	ECO	Financial Position
38	ECILF	Earnings $ per share
39	EECN	P-E Ratio; Earnings $ per share
40	ECL	Earnings $ per share
41	EEA	Earnings $ per share; Interim Earnings
42	EDGC	P-E Ratio; Earnings $ per share
43	EBS	Earnings $ per share
44	EDO	Earnings $ per share
45	ESPC	P-E Ratio; Earnings $ per share
46	AGE	Earnings $ per share

WAG YR 5 (If this figure is missing, use Last 12 mos. and mark *)
TOTAL WAG
÷6 or 10 (If all WAG columns are filled in, divide by 10; if WAG YR 2 has a dash in it, divide by 6)
P/E ÷ WAG (See Chapter 2, Section C)
(Total) POINTS

Figure 3.2 shows the form you will be using. When this is completed, you will have an alphabetical listing of approximately five percent of the soundest growth stocks traded. We now have the tough job of trimming this list down; however, we have at least succeeded in choosing the semi-finalists!

Section B: Awarding Points

At this stage, in order to continue the process of elimination, assign a numerical value to each stock listed. Points will be awarded for the factors discussed in Chapter 2 and listed in Section F of that chapter.

1. Weighted Average Growth (WAG): Total Possible Points = 45
    We have learned that growth in earnings is the most important factor in propelling a stock to higher prices. We also know that our formula for measuring the momentum of growth, WAG, gives us a realistic idea of the potential of the company to maintain their rate of increased earnings. We now allocate the greatest number of points which can be earned by a stock based on its Weighted Average Growth.

If the WAG is:	Points
65 or less	5
65.1 to 74	10
74.1 to 89	15
89.1 to 98	20
98.1 to 107	25

If the WAG is:	Points
107.1 to 115	30
115.1 to 123	35
123.1 to 131	40
131.1 and over	45

2. P/E Ratio: Total Possible Points = 25

It has been pointed out that a relatively low P/E ratio means that the stock has been priced cheaply by the investment community. Thus the combination of a high WAG and a low P/E ratio means that the potential for a large appreciation in the stock is present. We shall therefore assign the next largest possible number of points to this factor.

If P/E Ratio is:	Points
Over 21	0
21	.5
20	1.0
19	1.5
18	3.0
17	4.5
16	6.0
15	7.5
14	9.0
13	10.5
12	12.0
11	13.5
10	15.0
9	16.5
8	18.0
7	19.5
6	21.0
5	22.5
4	24.0
3 or less	25.0

Figure 3.2

* = Last 12 month

	SYMBOL	NAME OF STOCK	RTG.	EXCH.	INDUSTRY	P/E	YIELD	END F/Y	EARNINGS 1 19__	EARNINGS 2 19__
1										
2										
3										
4										
5										
6										
7										
8										
9										
10										
11										
12										
13										
14										
15										
16										
17										
18										
19										
20										
21										
22										
23										
24										
25										

Figure 3.2 continued

PER SHARE			WAG					÷ 6 or 10	P/E ÷ WAG	POINTS
3	4	5	YR 2	YR 3	YR 4	YR 5	TOTAL	WAG		
19___	19___	19___ OR*								

3. P/E as a % of WAG: Total Possible Points = 15
    Note: To figure this percentage, divide the P/E
    Ratio by the WAG, for example,

    P/E = 11; WAG = 28.9.
    11 ÷ 28.9 = 38.06; round off to 38.1%

This factor keeps the two ratings (P/E and WAG) in
proper perspective. In reality, it serves to modify the P/E
Ratio and has the effect of adding additional points. We
are assigning a total of 25 + 15 = 40 points in attempting
to find stocks at fair or bargain prices.

%	Points
Over 40%	0
35.1 to 40	2.5
30.1 to 35	5.0
27.5 to 30	7.5
22.5 to 27.4	10.0
Under 22.5	15.0

4. Dividend Yield: Total Possible Points = 10
    As mentioned in Section D of Chapter 2, rapid
    growth produces a great strain on cash flow.
    This means that most of the companies you
    select for purchase will have little or no money
    remaining for payment of dividends. Since you
    might be holding the stocks you purchase for
    extended periods of time, we shall give some
    credit to the dividend yield in our stock selection
    process.

% Dividend	Points
0 to .4	0
.5 to .9	2
1.0 to 2.0	4
2.1 to 3.0	6
3.1 to 4.0	8
4.1 & over	10

5. S&P Rating: Total Possible Points = 5
    The factors for which points have been awarded

thus far cover the main features in which we are interested. Since the ratings given by Standard & Poor's Corporation take certain additional factors into consideration, we shall award a small number of points based on their overall financial rating of the company. You will note that "NR" (not rated, or no ranking) is accorded the same number of points as B+, which is an average rating. The reason for this is that the NR rating is neither favorable nor unfavorable. As stated in the Stock Guide: "NR signifies no ranking because of insufficient data or because the stock is not amenable to the ranking process."

If Rating is:	Points
D	0
C	.8
B–	1.5
B	2.2
B+ or NR	2.9
A–	3.6
A	4.3
A+	5.0

Our next task is to figure the total points for each stock and enter in the "Points" column. An example is given below:

Factor	Value	Points
WAG	44.8	5.0
P/E	13	10.5
P/E as % of WAG	29%	7.5
Yield	1.0%	4.0
S&P rating	A	4.3
	Total Points	31.3

Now we shall list the top 20% (and ties) of the point scores. If you have 212 stocks, you would list the 42 stocks (212 x 20% = 42.4) with the greatest number of points. Prepare a form similar to Figure 3.3 with these columns:

Figure 3.3

FINAL POINT SCORE SUMMARY

Symbol	Name of Stock	Exch.	Ind.	Total Points	Orig. Price	Curr. Price	Adj. Points

SYMBOL

STOCK

EXCHANGE

INDUSTRY (Use Code Number as shown in Appendix A)

TOTAL POINTS

ORIGINAL PRICE (Price shown in the "Last" column in the "Last Sale Or Bid" section in the same month Stock Guide you used to obtain your data.)

CURRENT PRICE (Closing price of the stock at the end of the most recent market day)

ADJUSTED POINTS (Enter to nearest whole number)

The Adjusted Points are figured like this:

1. Divide the Original Price by the Current Price
2. Multiply the result by the Total Points.
   For example:

Original Price: $30.5 ÷
Current Price: $33.125
= 92.07% (rounded off to .921)

.921 x Total Points of 62.7
= 57.7 adjusted points
Round off to the nearest whole number:
58 Adjusted Points.

Section C:
The Final Selection

We have been very careful to select not only rapidly growing companies, but also well-managed ones with fairly priced stocks. One other step is necessary to be certain that our investments will be as safe as possible: diversification.

Diversification is an important part of investing. Industries have always been subject to falling into or out of favor with the investment community. Auto stocks might be "hot" for a few years and will climb to high prices, as evidenced by their P/E ratios. Then they fall out of favor and sell at depressed prices for a long period of time. The same holds true for virtually every industry.

Because of this phenomenon, we shall protect ourselves by adhering to the diversification table below:*

No. of Stocks Bought	Maximum No. In Same Industry
5 to 7	1
8 to 10	2
11 to 14	3
15 or more	4

Bearing this in mind, the final choice is quite simple. Let's say you plan to invest $25,000. Referring to the investment chart at the end of this section, you will choose twelve stocks and eventually buy eight of them. As the table above indicates, with the purchase of eight stocks you do not choose more than two in the same industry.

Pick the twelve stocks with the highest number of points. If more than two are in the same industry, eliminate the excess stocks from consideration and continue down the list until you have twelve stocks with the highest points, but no more than two in the same industry.

Amount You Plan To Invest		Eliminate Down To	Number Of
From	To	This Many Stocks	Stocks To Buy
$10,000	$14,999	9	5
15,000	19,999	10	6
20,000	24,999	11	7
25,000	29,999	12	8
30,000	34,999	13	9
35,000	39,999	14	10
40,000	44,999	15	11
45,000	59,999	16	12
60,000	79,999	17	13
80,000	100,000	18	14

* Each $25,000 over $100,000, add one stock to each column.

---

* Since Industry Code No. 48 is a catch-all for miscellaneous industries, the Diversification Table applies to all industry codes except this one.

You will discover a bit further on the reason for the "Eliminate Down to This Many Stocks" column.

Section D: Stock Purchases

Now it's time to visit your broker. I suggest that you use a full-service broker for this system rather than a discount broker. The reasons are (1) you will occasionally need to obtain information and consult with your broker, and (2) this is not an in-and-out system where commission costs will seriously erode profits.

If you don't have a broker at this time, a couple of tips might be helpful. First, be sure the firm has a research department or access to research. Some smaller or regional firms purchase their research materials from the larger national brokerage houses.

Second, don't be afraid to ask a full-service broker for a discount. Depending on your activity and the size of your account, a 10% to 25% discount is not unreasonable.

Ask your broker to check the eight stocks you plan to buy. Check the current price and any other information that might affect your decision. Perhaps there is news that the company might be taken over by another; perhaps they just came out with a new earnings report, showing a decrease.

This information can be checked in a matter of seconds on a computer screen. If there is any news which makes you decide not to buy the stock, simply substitute another from the four reserve stocks.

Now place your buy orders "at the market." I nearly always use market orders, except for the special situation explained below. If you are buying a stock, chosen after careful research or through a process of elimination such as described in this book, it makes little significant difference whether the price you pay is $60 or $61 per share.

There is a certain circumstance in which you would definitely want to place a limit order. Your broker can be helpful in this situation. Let's say that one of your selections for purchase is Company R, a thinly traded over-the-counter stock. The bid price on which you based your Point Score calculation was 6 1/2 dollars. Upon checking the price, your broker notices it is 6 1/2 bid, 8 7/8 asked.

A market order would probably result in your paying 8 7/8, or 35% more than you planned to pay. True, it's only 2 3/8 dollars, but percentage-wise, it's exactly the same as paying $54 per share for a stock that you planned to buy for $40!

Where there is a spread of more than 10% in the bid and asked price, compute how much you can pay for the stock without lowering its Point Score sufficiently to disqualify it as a candidate for purchase.

Let's say you plan to buy six stocks. The sixth highest stock on your list has 82 points. Company R at 6 1/2 dollars is third on your list with 103 points. Your problem is to figure how much you can pay for the stock without lowering its Point Score below 82.

This is the only place in the book where it is necessary to use a little elementary algebra. Our formula is:

A is to B as X is to C, expressed algebraically as

$$A:B = X:C$$

A = Price at which you computed the Point Score of the stock
  (6 1/2 in this example)

B = Point Score of lowest stock that qualifies for purchase (82 in this example)

C = Point Score of stock you wish to purchase (103 in this example)

X = Highest price per share that you can pay.

$$A:B = X:C$$

(A is 6.5) : (B is 82) = (X is unknown) : (C is 103)

Stated another way:

$$\frac{6.5}{82} \qquad \frac{X}{103}$$

Next, cross multiply:	$(82)(X)$	$=$	$(6.5)(103)$
This equals:	$82\ X$	$=$	669.5
Divide both sides by 82:	X	$=$	8.16

You can pay up to 8.16 (8 1/8) for the stock of Company R. Instruct your broker to buy Company R at 8 1/8 dollars, limit price. If you are unable to buy the stock at this price by the next day, cancel the order and substitute another from the reserve stocks.

All purchases should be in even hundred shares (round lots) with approximately the same amount of dollars invested in each stock. There will, however, be situations where it won't be possible to invest a similar dollar amount in each stock. For example, let's say you want to invest $13,000. The table on page 34 tells you to buy five stocks. The top five stocks in point score are:

	Current Price
Stock #1	11 1/2
Stock #2	59
Stock #3	27 1/8
Stock #4	14
Stock #5	7 3/4

Since you are investing $13,000 in five stocks, you will put as close as possible to $2,600 in each stock.* You must buy in round lots of one hundred shares, so the minimum investment in Stock #2 is $5,900. What you must do is deduct $5,900 from $13,000, leaving you with $7,100 to invest in the four remaining stocks, or as close to $1,775 as possible in each stock.

Now you need $2,713 for Stock #3. Deduct this from $7,100, leaving $4,387 for the remaining stocks, or $1,462 per stock. You would buy:

			Amount Remaining
Stock #1	100 shares=	$1,150	$3,237
Stock #4	100 shares=	1,400	1,837
Stock #5	200 shares=	1,550	287

The remaining amount of $287 may be left in your account.

---

* To simplify the above example, commissions were not included.

Section E: An Illustration of the System

The following is an illustration of the stock selection system. Checking the data and doing the calculations will increase understanding of how the system works. Notice the following two modifications employed for purposes of simplification.

1. Instead of going through the entire Stock Guide, which would give us several hundred candidates for purchase, we shall only go through the letter "A". As shown in Figure 3.4, we end up with twenty stocks. (The October, 1990 issue of the Stock Guide was used for this illustration.)

2. Instead of listing the top 20% in point score (which would be just four stocks), we shall list the top 75%, or 15 stocks.

It will be assumed that you wish to invest $18,000. The table below shows that you must eliminate down to ten stocks and actually buy six.

Figure 3.4 is a listing of the twenty stocks that qualify as candidates for purchase. Check the information carefully and duplicate the calculations. If your computations result in a different total Point Score, review the chapter and try again.

Figure 3.5 is a work sheet which will facilitate the computation of Total Points. Enter the points for each factor (S & P Rating, P/E, etc.) on the work sheet. After you total the points, transfer this total to the last column in Figure 3.4 (since the totals are already entered in Figure 3.4, check to see if your totals agree.)

The top 75% (15 stocks) in point score have been entered in Figure 3.6. Since we are going to buy six stocks, we must not have more than one in the same industry, except as noted previously (Industry Code 48, Miscellaneous). We will pick the top ten stocks in Adjusted Point Score, the last four being the substitutes.

	SYMBOL	INDUSTRY	POINTS	PRICE
1.	AALR	10	73	7
2.	ATM	35	47	14 3/4
3.	ACAT	48	42	7 1/8
4.	ABRI	48	41	2 3/4
5.	ARDNA	9	40	47
6.	APCC	32	32	14
7.	AMZ	48	32	17 1/2
8.	ACRCA	27	26	8 3/4
9.	AEX	24	24	14 7/8
10.	APOG	21	21	16 3/4

This list is based on the computations and total scores. It eliminates all duplications in the same industry (except Code 48).

Once the stock selection is completed, calculate the number of shares to be purchased for a total of 18,000 dollars (for this example). The quantity calculations should leave some money available for commissions. If this illustration were a real situation, the next step would be to visit the stockbroker.

Ask the broker to check for news stories or recent earnings reports. If this new information eliminates one or more of the top six choices, simply recalculate and select an alternative from the list.

All that remains in the selection process is to place the round lot buy orders "at the market." The selection system has provided a list of stocks which have a reasonable chance to provide some future profits.

Section F: Summary

1. Use the S & P Stock Guide. Put a dash by the stocks that fulfill the following qualifications:

    a. They are not preferred stocks.

    b. They are not ADR stocks.

    c. They show no earnings decrease in 6-mo. or 9-mo. interim earnings.

    d. They show an earnings increase each year and

Figure 3.4

* = Last 12 month

	SYMBOL	NAME OF STOCK	RTG.	EXCH.	INDUSTRY	P/E	YIELD	END F/Y	EARNINGS	
									1986	1987*
1	ABRI	Abrams Industries	B	OTC	48	10	5.7	Apr.	.20	.33
2	ACN	Acason Corp.	B–	NY	2	23	–0–	Dec.	.27	.49
3	ADBE	Adobe Systems	NR	OTC	10	11	1.3	Nov.	.19	.42
4	AALR	Advanced Logic Research	NR	OTC	10	5	–0–	Sep.	.03	.11
5	AEX	Air Express Int'l	B–	AS	24	7	–0–	Dec.	.82	1.52
6	ACV	Alberto Culver, Cl.B	A–	NY	33	16	1.0	Sep.	.34	.64
7	AIDC	Aldus Corp	NR	OTC	10	21	–0–	Dec.	.21	.66
8	AEWS	Allwaste Inc.	NR	OTC	12	15	–0–	Aug.	.12	.77
9	ALTR	Altera Corp.	NR	OTC	10	16	–0–	Dec.	0.25	.07
10	ACRCA	Am. Capital REsearch "A"	NR	OTC	27	15	–0–	Feb.	.07	.15
11	AMZ	American List	B+	AS	48	12	1.0	Feb.	.54	.67
12	APCC	Am. Power Conversion	NR	OTC	32	18	–0–	Dec.	.06	.39
13	AMSWA	Am. Software, Ci.A	B+	OTC	10	10	3.1	Apr.	.26	.38
14	ANLY	Analysts Int'l	B	OTC	10	9	5.1	Jun.	4.22	.33
15	ATM	Anthem Electronics	B+	NY	35	10	–0–	Dec.	.28	.50
16	APOG	Apogee Enterprises	A–	OTC	21	12	1.7	Feb.	.32	.87
17	AAPL	Apple Computer	B+	OTC	10	8	1.5	Sep.	1.19	1.65
18	ACAT	Arctco Inc.	NR	OTC	48	6	–0–	Mar.	.18	.58
19	ARDNA	Arden Group Ci."A"	B	OTC	9	6	–0–	Dec.	1.89	3.76
20	ACAD	Autodesk, Inc.	NR	OTC	10	18	1.0	Jan.	.55	.89
21										
22										
23										
24										
25										

Figure 3.4 continued

| PER SHARE | | | WAG | | | | | +6 or 10 | | |
1988	1989	1990 OR*	YR 2	YR 3	YR 4	YR 5	TOTAL	WAG	P/E + WAG	POINTS
.36	.48	.51	65%	18%	100%	25%	208%	20.8%	48%	32.2
.78	1.07	1.20*	81	118	112	49	360	36.0	64	6.5
.98	1.55	1.75*	121	267	174	52	614	61.4	18	48.9
.36	.41	1.22*	200	400	42	790	1432	143.2	3	85.4
1.64	1.70	1.95*	85	16	11	59	171	17.1	41	26.0
.99	1.12	1.33	88	109	39	75	311	31.1	51	18.6
1.15	1.21	1.26*	200	148	16	77	381	38.1	55	8.4
.27	.40	.44*	42	118	144	40	344	34.4	44	15.4
.38	.55	.62*	—	200	89	38	327	54.5	29	21.4
.46	.57	.60*	114	400	72	21	607	60.7	25	25.4
.76	1.45	1.57*	24	27	272	33	356	35.6	34	28.9
.94	1.70	2.10*	200	282	243	94	819	81.9	22	35.9
.45	.64	.82	46	37	127	113	323	32.3	31	35.9
.69	1.09	1.29	—	109	116	55	280	46.7	19	48.7
1.00	1.39	1.85*	79	200	117	132	528	52.8	19	37.2
1.00	1.04	1.19*	172	30	12	58	272	27.2	44	24.6
3.08	3.53	3.65	39	173	44	14	270	27.0	30	37.4
.79	1.13	1.17*	200	72	129	14	415	41.5	14	43.9
6.27	7.21	7.12*	99	130	48	28	305	30.5	20	43.2
1.35	1.91	2.30	62	103	124	82	377	37.1	49	14.9

Figure 3.5

POINT SCORE WORK SHEET

SYMBOL	RATING	P/E	P/E%	YIELD	WAG	TOT. PTS

Figure 3.6

FINAL POINT SCORE SUMMARY

Symbol	Name of Stock	Exch.	Ind.	Total Points	Orig. Price	Curr. Price	Adj. Points
AALR	Advanced Logic Research	OTC	10	85.4	6	7	73
ADBE	Adobe systems	OTC	10	48.9	19	25 1/2	36
ANLY	Analysts Int'l.	OTC	10	48.7	11	12	45
ACAT	Arcto Inc.	OTC	48	43.9	6 7/8	7 1/8	42
ARDNA	Arden Group, Cl"A"	OTC	9	43.2	44	47	40
AAPL	Apple Computer	OTC	10	37.4	29	35 1/4	31
ATM	Anthem Electronics	NY	35	37.2	18 3/8	14 3/4	47
APCC	Amer. Power Conversion	OTC	32	35.9	37 1/4	42*	32
AMSWA	Amer. Softwear, Cl"A"	OTC	10	35.9	7 3/4	10 3/8	27
ABRI	Abrams Industries	OTC	48	32.2	3 1/2	2 3/4	41
AMZ	American List	AS	48	28.9	19 3/8	17 1/2	32
AEX	Air Express Int'l.	AS	24	26.0	13 7/8	14 7/8	24
ACRCA	Am. Capital Research "A"	OTC	27	25.4	9 1/8	8 3/4	26
APOG	Apogee Enterprises	OTC	21	24.6	14 1/2	16 3/4	21
ALTR	Altera Corp.	OTC	10	21.4	10	9 1/4	23

NOTE: All prices are bid. There will be large spreads between the bid and asked price on some of the thinly traded stocks. Be sure your broker checks this out before placing your buy orders. Then refer to page 35 and 36.

*Actual price is 14; stock split 3 for 1 on 9/28/90.

have at least doubled their earnings.

  e. The number of preferred shares does not exceed 10% of the number of common shares outstanding.

  f. Current assets exceed current liabilities by at least 25%.

  g. The P/E Ratio is not more than twice that of the Dow Jones Industrial Average.

2. List the stocks alphabetically that you have marked.

3. Award points to each stock. The total possible points are 100.

4. Enter the total points by each stock in the "Total Points" column.

5. List the highest 20% of point score and ties.

6. Determine how much you wish to invest and refer to the investment table.

7. Don't select more stocks in any one industry than called for by the diversification table.

8. Have your broker check your stocks and substitute alternates if necessary.

9. Place your orders "at the market," in round lots (hundred share amounts).

The Ultra-Conservative Investor

In Section E, Chapter 2, it was pointed out that one of the selection factors to be given consideration is the S & P rating, which rates the investment quality of a stock.

Out of approximately 4,700 stocks in the Standard and Poor's Stock Guide, only 112 — or slightly more than 2% received the highest rating of A+. Moreover, because of the conservative nature of these stocks, only twelve of them even qualified as candidates for purchase. In almost every case, the reason they did not qualify is that earnings had not doubled from Year 1 to Year 5.

Nevertheless, although statistics are unavailable to prove this point, it would be safe to assume that no A+ rated stock has ever failed. The reason for this is not that this (or any other) rating system is infallible, but that, before failing, signs of weakness in the company would appear that would cause Standard and Poor's to downrate the stock from A+ to a lower rating.

The purpose of the above discussion is to make this point: the method of stock selection described thus far will provide a list of fast growing, dynamic companies. Some of these companies will not be well known; in fact, it is quite probable that even your stock broker may not be aware of them until now. Companies such as these might be a concern to the very conservative investor.

How, then, should this type of investor proceed? There are two viable methods.

Purchase Only A+ Rated Stocks

Before beginning the six steps for stock selection (Chapter 3, Section A), check the stock rating column of the Standard and Poor's Stock Guide. Unless the rating is A+, proceed immediately to the next stock. If the stock has an A+ rating, proceed with the selection process, placing a dash by stocks qualifying as candidates.

Now select the stocks the very same way as you did in Chapter 3. These stocks will not have as high a point score, but you will have the security of knowing that they are rated among the very highest quality of all stocks.

Since there will be so few A+ rated stocks that qualify, you will have to adjust the table showing the amount to invest and number of stocks to buy, as shown in Chapter 3, Section C, to the table below:

Amount You Plan To Invest		Eliminate Down To This Many Stocks	Number Of Stocks To Buy
From	*To*		
$10,000	$19,999	5	3
20,000	29,999	6	4
30,000	39,999	7	5
40,000	59,999	8	6
60,000	79,999	9	7
80,000	100,000	10	8

*Each $25,000 over $100,000, add one stock to each column.

It will also be necessary to revise the Diversification Table shown on page 34, since it is likely that you will be buying a smaller number of stocks. If you purchase A+ rated stocks only, use the the Diversification Table shown below:*

No. Stocks Bought	Maximum No. in Same Industry
3 to 4	1
5 to 6	2
7 to 8	3
9 or more	4

*Since Industry Code No. 48 is a catch-all for miscellaneous industries, the Diversification Table applies to all industries except this one.

Use a Combination System

The purpose of the method described below is to provide the investor with a combination of safety and maximum growth potential. A minimum investment of $20,000 is required, to be invested as follows:

A. Invest a portion of your total investment (minimum $10,000) exactly as described in Chapter 3. The stocks you purchase should be held in street name by the brokerage firm, as this facilitates and expedites the trades you will be making.

B. Invest the remaining portion (minimum $10,000) in A+ rated stocks, with the intention of holding these stocks for the long term. Take delivery of the stock certificates.

   The A+ rated stocks would be managed the same way as the others, with one very important exception: the stocks are to be sold only if the S & P rating falls below A+.

For those investors with substantial amounts to put into the stock market, this system provides a great deal of flexibility. Should you desire to stress safety, you might wish to place 60% or 70% or more of your funds in A+ rated stocks. If, on the other hand, you wish to emphasize growth, the greater percentage of your funds would be invested as outlined in Chapter 3.

Stock Sales and Additional 5 Purchases

Section A: Stock Sheet

A few days after purchasing your stocks, you will receive a confirmation from your brokerage firm for each stock you bought. This will show your account number, the trade date, settlement date, number of shares, price per share, dollar amount, other costs such as commission and transfer fee, and net dollar amount.

Prepare a Stock Sheet (Figure 5.1) for each stock:

1. Enter the information called for on the top line.

2. Under "Price Record" write the current year on the YEAR line. Enter the price as the year progresses.

3. Under "Earnings":

   a. Insert the month that the Fiscal Year ends.

   b. Using the original listing you prepared (Figure 3.2), enter the earnings for the past five years. If you used the "Last 12 mos." for the current year, enter this figure in pencil. Then, when the current year's

Figure 5.1

STOCK SHEET

SYMBOL	STOCK	EXCHANGE	ACCT. NO.

SPLITS, STOCK DIVIDENDS, OTHER NEWS: _____

_____

_____

_____

_____

_____

_____

PRICE RECORD

YEAR											
March 31											
June 30											
Sept. 30											
Dec. 31											

EARNINGS (F/Y END:)

YEAR											
EARNINGS											
WTD. AVE.											
POINTS											

BUY/SELL DATA

TRADE DATE	SH. BOT.	PRICE	AMOUNT	TOTAL AMOUNT	AVERAGE PRICE

TRADE DATE	SH. SOLD	PRICE	AMOUNT	GAIN	LOSS

REASON FOR SALE:

earnings become available, erase this figure and enter the current year.

   c. Enter the WAG under the current year.

   d. Enter the Adjusted Total Points under the current year.

4. Under "Buy/Sell Data":

   a. Enter trade date, number of shares bought and price per share.

   b. In the "Amount" column, enter the exact amount (e.g., 3212.60).

   c. In the "Total Amount" column, enter the amount rounded off to the nearest dollar.

   d. Divide the Total Amount by the number of shares and enter under "Average Price"; carry to two decimal places (e.g., you bought 300 shares for \$3,213; 3213 ÷ 300 = 10.71). If additional shares are bought in the future, or if there is a stock dividend or split, enter in this section and recompute the average price per share.

Section B: Summary Sheet

The Summary Sheet (Figure 5.2) is a record of all transactions in your account that affect the cash balance — stock purchases and sales, deposits to and withdrawals from the account, dividends received, any interest paid by the brokerage firm on cash balances in your account, etc. Prepare the Summary Sheet as follows:

1. Directly under "Balance For'd", above the double line, enter the amount deposited with the brokerage firm.

2. Fill in the trade date, stock symbol, number of shares bought and price per share for each purchase.

3. Fill in the total amount to the nearest dollar.

4. Deduct the amount from the "Balance For'd" figure.

Figure 5.2

Acct. No. _____   Page _____

SUMMARY SHEET

DATE 19__	STOCK SYMBOL	SHARES BOT.	SOLD	PRICE	AMOUNT	OTHER*	INC.	EXP.	BALANCE FOR'D: $

*1 = Dividend   4 =
2 = Deposit   5 =
3 = Withdrawal   6 =

5. List the next stock the same way, deducting the amount from the previous "Balance For'd" figure.

6. Continue until you have listed all the stocks you bought.

When you receive your monthly brokerage statement, enter *total* dividends received and add this to the Balance. Enter the date of the statement, the amount and a "1" under "Other" to show it was dividends. Add the amount entered under Income to the Balance. Any other transactions that add to or subtract from your cash balance will be entered on this form.

Section C: Dividend Record

Assuming the stocks are being held in "street name" by the brokerage house, you will know what dividends have been paid from the monthly statements. Enter these dividends by company on the Dividend Record (Figure 5.3), then enter the total dividends received on the Summary Sheet.

Section D:
Weekly Price Chart

Prepare the Weekly Price Chart (Figure 5.4) as follows:

1. List the symbols of all stocks purchased and the exchange where each stock is traded.

2. Beginning with the Friday, immediately following the day on which you bought the stocks, enter the dates (e.g., 3/9 - 3/16 - 3/23 - 3/20 - 4/6, etc.).

3. In the column Buy Price/Shares, enter these figures: e.g., $\frac{13\ 1/2}{300}$.
    These figures would be entered in pencil in order to adjust the average price and quantity when additional shares are purchased.

4. The "Stop" column has the greatest importance on the Weekly Price Chart. The price entered

Figure 5.3

DIVIDEND RECORD

SYMBOL	DATE	AMOUNT		SYMBOL	DATE	AMOUNT

Figure 5.4

WEEKLY PRICE CHART

STOCK SYMBOL	EXCH.	WEEK ENDING (19___):								BUY PRICE SHARES	STOP

STOCK SYMBOL	EXCH.	WEEK ENDING (19___):								BUY PRICE SHARES	STOP

will be a signal to sell if the stock price is dropping. Enter a price in the stop column, based on the stop formula in the following table. If the closing Friday price is at or below the price in the stop column, *contact the broker on Monday morning and sell the stock.*

IMPORTANT: If you find that you don't have the will power to sell if a stock hits the stop price, enter a "sell stop" order with the broker. The order should be entered GTC (Good Till Cancelled).

A sell stop order is a sell order placed at a specific price. When the stated price is traded on or through the sell stop order becomes a market sell order and is executed at the best available price. Most brokerage firms are currently not able to accept stop orders on any over-the-counter (OTC) stocks.

A sell stop order has volatility risk. Many times the price of a stock can drop just low enough to activate the stop and climb right back to its former level. But, it can be better to use a sell stop order than fail to sell as a stock price is dropping.

Brokerage firms have different policies regarding the length of time they will carry a GTC order. Be sure to ask how long the order will remain in effect and make a note of its expiration.

The following table gives guidelines for the calculation of a sell stop price.

PURCHASE PRICE (Or Weekly Close, if Higher)	SELL IF PRICE DROPS:
Under 5	40%
5 1/8 to 10	30%
10 1/8 to 20	25%
20 1/8 to 35	20%
35 1/8 to 70	15%
Over 70	10%

Use a pencil to make your entries in the "Stop" column. When you enter the Friday closing price, check the "Buy Price" in the column next to the "Stop" column. If the Friday closing price is higher, re-figure the stop, erase the former figure and enter the higher one. *Remember*: you continue to raise the stop as the weekly closing prices go up, but *seldom lower the stop*.

There are three situations requiring a lowered stop.

A. Section F of this chapter deals with additional purchases. When more shares of a stock are purchased, the average price for all shares is figured. You then re-compute your stop based on this price. In some cases this will result in lowering the stop.

B. Another lowered stop situation is when a stock splits. The new stop is based on the price of the stock on the first Friday close after the split becomes effective. If an order was entered with a broker the firm will either automatically adjust the stop for a split or the order will be cancelled. Check your brokerage firm's policy on handling GTC orders during a split or a dividend payment.

C. The third exception applies only to stocks that pay a dividend. When you record the weekly closing price of your stocks, you will sometimes see an "x" after the amount of the dividend. This means that the stock went ex-dividend during the week. In other words, the person who sold the stock on ex-date is entitled to the dividend, even if the stock is sold before the dividend is actually paid.

Before you instruct your broker to sell the stock, add in the amount of the dividend. If the price is still at or below your stop, then sell; otherwise, don't sell unless the stock is at your stop price the following week. Use Table 5.1 to determine how much to add in to the price if the stock went ex-dividend.

Table 5.1

DIVIDEND			POINTS
.01	to	.125¢	1/8
.126	to	.25¢	1/4
.251	to	.375¢	3/8
.376	to	.50¢	1/2
.501	to	.625¢	5/8
.626	to	.75¢	3/4
.751	to	.875¢	7/8
.876	to	$1.00	1
1.01	to	$1.125	1 1/8
1.126	to	$1.25	1 1/4

For example, you own a stock; the stop on the form is 31 1/2. The dividend is .30¢. Referring to the above table, you note that this represents 3/8 of a dollar. The week the stock goes ex-dividend, the weekly closing price is 31 3/8. Before you call your broker to sell, add back the 3/8 to 31 3/8, which gives you 31 3/4, so you would not sell. If the price the following week closes at 31 1/2 or lower, then you would sell.

Appendix B illustrates the quickest way to re-figure your stop. IMPORTANT: In addition to the stop, there are three other conditions which would cause you to sell a stock:

a. When you enter the annual earnings on the Stock Sheet, sell immediately if they don't show an increase over the prior year.

b. After entering the annual earnings—assuming that they show an increase—re-figure the points. If you chose stocks as shown in Chapter 3, sell the stock if total points are less than 30. If you chose the A+ rated stocks, sell if total points are less than fifteen.

c. If you use this system for several years, you will likely see one or more of your stocks suddenly jump a few dollars higher. On checking with your broker, you discover that there are strong rumors of another company seeking to buy it out.

As an example, let's say that "B", which you bought at 16 3/8, suddenly jumps to 23 in a week. You phone your broker and find out that the company has received a buyout offer at $23.50 per share. A spokesman for "B" says that another company is also interested in buying at a higher price, they think the offer of 23 1/2 is too low. What do you do?

Each situation will be different; have your broker obtain sufficient information so you can make an informed decision. This informational need is a reason to use a full-service broker.

Section E:
Continuing the Illustration

To be certain you understand how to set up the system once you have made your purchases, the illustration given in Section E, Chapter 3 will be continued.

For the sake of simplicity and clarity, we shall make the following assumptions:
1. You were successful in purchasing the first six stocks on your list (page 39).
2. You paid exactly the price quoted on the list.
3. Commissions came to 3% of the cost on all purchases.

With $18,000 to invest in six stocks, you wanted to invest $3,000 per stock or as close to this figure as possible. Since 100 shares of ARDNA will cost more than $3,000, we shall list it first. The balance remaining is $13,159. Dividing that amount by five, we find that we have an average of $2,632 to invest in the remaining stocks. See Table 5.2.

A few days after making these purchases, you receive the confirmations from the brokerage house. The first thing to do is to check the figures for accuracy. Call the broker if there are any discrepancies.

Table 5.2

Symbol	Price	Shares	Amt	Commission	Total	Balance
ARDNA	47	100	$4,700	$141.00	$4,841.00	$13,159.00
AALR	7	400	2,800	84.00	2,884.00	10,275.00
ATM	14 3/4	200	2,950	88.50	3,038.50	7,236.50
ACAT	7 1/8	400	2,850	85.50	2,935.50	4,301.00
ABRI	2 3/4	900	2,475	74.25	2,549.25	1,751.75
APCC	14	100	1,400	42.00	1,442.00	309.75

Now the Summary Sheet is prepared (Figure 5.5). Notice that the figures shown on this form are to the nearest dollar. When you receive your monthly brokerage statements, check to see that the cash balance in your account is the same (within a couple of dollars) as the balance shown on your Summary Sheet. If it isn't, phone your broker to find out why.

Next, prepare a Stock Sheet for each of the six stocks (Figures 5.6 through 5.11). Note the following:

1. Under "EARNINGS" the asterisk signifies that the 1990 earnings figure is not yet available, so the "Last 12 mos" figure is entered in pencil. This will be replaced with the 1990 earnings as soon as that figure is available.

2. Under "BUY/SELL DATA" the figure in the "AMOUNT" column is in dollars and cents; the figure in the "TOTAL AMOUNT" column is to the nearest dollar. The "AVERAGE PRICE" is the "TOTAL AMOUNT" divided by the "SH. BOT.".

Now prepare the Weekly Price Chart (Figure 5.12).

1. Enter the figures in the "BUY PRICE/SHARES" column in pencil. When you sell a stock and buy additional shares in other stocks currently owned, draw a line through the stock that was sold. Change the Buy Price to the average price per share of the stock(s) in which you bought additional shares. Change "SHARES" to the total shares now owned.

Figure 5.5

Acct. No. _543210_

SUMMARY SHEET

DATE 19<u>90</u>	STOCK SYMBOL	SHARES BOT.	SHARES SOLD	PRICE	AMOUNT	OTHER* INC.	EXP.	BALANCE FOR'D: $18,000
12-1	ARDNA	100		47	4,841			13,159
	AALR	400		7	2,884			10,275
	ATM	200		14 ¾	3,039			7,236
	ACAT	400		7 ⅛	2,936			4,300
	ABRI	900		2 ¾	2,549			1,751
	APCC	100		14	1,442			309

*1 = Dividend	4 =
2 = Deposit	5 =
3 = Withdrawal	6 =

Figure 5.6

STOCK SHEET

SYMBOL	STOCK	EXCHANGE	ACCT. NO.
ABRI	*Abrams Industries*	*OTC*	*543210*

SPLITS, STOCK DIVIDENDS, OTHER NEWS: _____

_____

_____

_____

_____

_____

_____

PRICE RECORD

YEAR											
March 31											
June 30											
Sept. 30											
Dec. 31											

EARNINGS (F/Y END: *Apr.*)

YEAR	*1986*	*'87*	*'88*	*'89*	*'90*						
EARNINGS	*.20*	*.33*	*.36*	*.48*	*.51*						
WTD. AVE.					*20.8*						
POINTS					*41*						

BUY/SELL DATA

TRADE DATE	SH. BOT.	PRICE	AMOUNT	TOTAL AMOUNT	AVERAGE PRICE
12-1-90	*900*	*2³/₄*	*2,549.25*	*2,549*	*2.83*

TRADE DATE	SH. SOLD	PRICE	AMOUNT	GAIN	LOSS

REASON FOR SALE:

Figure 5.7

STOCK SHEET

SYMBOL	STOCK	EXCHANGE	ACCT. NO.
AALR	*Advanced Logic Research*	*OTC*	*543210*

SPLITS, STOCK DIVIDENDS, OTHER NEWS: _____

_____
_____
_____
_____
_____
_____
_____

PRICE RECORD

YEAR											
March 31											
June 30											
Sept. 30											
Dec. 31											

EARNINGS (F/Y END: *Sept.*)

YEAR	*1986*	*'87*	*'88*	*'89*	*'90*					
EARNINGS	*.03*	*.11*	*.36*	*.41*	*1.22**					
WTD. AVE.					*143.2*					
POINTS					*73*					

BUY/SELL DATA

TRADE DATE	SH. BOT.	PRICE	AMOUNT	TOTAL AMOUNT	AVERAGE PRICE
12-1-90	*400*	*7*	*2,884.00*	*2,884*	*7.21*

TRADE DATE	SH. SOLD	PRICE	AMOUNT	GAIN	LOSS

REASON FOR SALE:

Figure 5.8

STOCK SHEET STOCK SHEET
STOCK SHEET

SYMBOL ATM	STOCK Anthem Electronics	EXCHANGE NYSE	ACCT. NO. 543210

SPLITS, STOCK DIVIDENDS, OTHER NEWS: _____

PRICE RECORD

YEAR											
March 31											
June 30											
Sept. 30											
Dec. 31											

EARNINGS (F/Y END: Dec.)

YEAR	1986	'87	'88	'89	'90						
EARNINGS	.28	.50	1.00	1.39	1.85*						
WTD. AVE.					52.8						
POINTS					47						

BUY/SELL DATA

TRADE DATE	SH. BOT.	PRICE	AMOUNT	TOTAL AMOUNT	AVERAGE PRICE
12-1-90	200	14 3/4	3,038.50	3,039	15.20

TRADE DATE	SH. SOLD	PRICE	AMOUNT	GAIN	LOSS

REASON FOR SALE:

Figure 5.9

STOCK SHEET

SYMBOL	STOCK	EXCHANGE	ACCT. NO.
ACAT	*Arctco Inc.*	*OTC*	*543210*

SPLITS, STOCK DIVIDENDS, OTHER NEWS: _____

_____

_____

_____

_____

_____

_____

_____

PRICE RECORD

YEAR												
March 31												
June 30												
Sept. 30												
Dec. 31												

EARNINGS (F/Y END: *Mar.*)

YEAR	*1986*	*'87*	*'88*	*'89*	*'90*					
EARNINGS	*.18*	*.58*	*.79*	*1.13*	*1.17*[*]					
WTD. AVE.					*41.5*					
POINTS					*42*					

BUY/SELL DATA

TRADE DATE	SH. BOT.	PRICE	AMOUNT	TOTAL AMOUNT	AVERAGE PRICE
12-1-90	*400*	*7 1/8*	*2,935.50*	*2,936*	*7.34*

TRADE DATE	SH. SOLD	PRICE	AMOUNT	GAIN	LOSS

REASON FOR SALE:

Figure 5.10

STOCK SHEET

SYMBOL	STOCK	EXCHANGE	ACCT. NO.
APCC	American Power Conversion	OTC	543210

SPLITS, STOCK DIVIDENDS, OTHER NEWS: _____

_____
_____
_____
_____
_____
_____

PRICE RECORD

YEAR											
March 31											
June 30											
Sept. 30											
Dec. 31											

EARNINGS (F/Y END: Dec.)

YEAR	1986	'87	'88	'89	'90						
EARNINGS	.06	.39	.94	1.70	2.10*						
WTD. AVE.					81.9						
POINTS					32						

BUY/SELL DATA

TRADE DATE	SH. BOT.	PRICE	AMOUNT	TOTAL AMOUNT	AVERAGE PRICE
12-1-90	100	14	1,442.00	1,442	14.42

TRADE DATE	SH. SOLD	PRICE	AMOUNT	GAIN	LOSS

REASON FOR SALE:

Figure 5.11

STOCK SHEET

SYMBOL	STOCK		EXCHANGE	ACCT. NO.
ARDNA	*Arden Group, Cl. "A"*		*OTC*	*543210*

SPLITS, STOCK DIVIDENDS, OTHER NEWS: _____

_____

_____

_____

_____

_____

_____

PRICE RECORD

YEAR											
March 31											
June 30											
Sept. 30											
Dec. 31											

EARNINGS (F/Y END: *Dec.*)

YEAR	*1986*	*'87*	*'88*	*'89*	*'90*						
EARNINGS	*1.89*	*3.76*	*6.21*	*7.21*	*7.72**						
WTD. AVE.					*30.5*						
POINTS					*40*						

BUY/SELL DATA

TRADE DATE	SH. BOT.	PRICE	AMOUNT	TOTAL AMOUNT	AVERAGE PRICE	
12-1-90	*100*	*47*	*4,841.00*	*4,841*	*48.41*	

TRADE DATE	SH. SOLD	PRICE	AMOUNT	GAIN	LOSS	

REASON FOR SALE:

Figure 5.12

WEEKLY PRICE CHART

STOCK SYMBOL	EXCH.	WEEK ENDING (19 _90_):_; 1991_								BUY PRICE ——— SHARES	STOP
		12/7	12/14	12/21	12/28	1/4	1/11	1/18	1/25		
ATM	NY									$14\,^3/_4$ ——— 200	$1\,^3/_8$
ABRI	OTC									$2\,^3/_4$ ——— 900	$1\,^{11}/_{16}$
AALR	OTC									7 ——— 400	5
APCC	OTC									14 ——— 100	$10\,^3/_4$
ACAT	OTC									$7\,^1/_8$ ——— 400	$5\,^1/_8$
ARDNA	OTC									47 ——— 100	$41\,^1/_8$

STOCK SYMBOL	EXCH.	WEEK ENDING (19___):								BUY PRICE ——— SHARES	STOP

2. Enter the "STOP" in pencil. In figuring the stop, take the price in the "AVERAGE PRICE" column of the Stock Sheet and multiply it by the figure shown in the table on page 56.

Here is how you would figure the initial stops on these six stocks (see Appendix B):

ATM: 15.20 x .75 = 11.40; round off to 11 3/8.
ABRI: 2.83 x .60 = 1.70; round off to 1 11/16.
AALR: 7.21 x .70 = 5.05; round off to 5.
APCC: 14.42 x .75 = 10.82; round off to 10 3/4.
ACAT: 7.34 x .70 = 5.14; round off to 5 1/8.
ARDNA: 48.41 x .85 = 41.15; round off to 41 1/8.

Section F:
Additional Purchases

As soon as you have sold one or more stocks in accordance with Section D of this chapter, you will want to reinvest the money in the remaining stocks. Use the guidelines below:

1. As with the original purchases, buy in hundred share round lots only.

2. Arrange the stocks still owned in order of point totals, highest to lowest. *Buy up to the original number of shares purchased*, if possible. For example:

   a. You have just sold one of your stocks — 200 shares at 37, for a net amount of $7,178. List the remaining stocks (see Figure 5.13):

Stock	Original Purchase	Current Points	Current Price
ABC	100 sh.	78	82 1/8
BCD	300 sh.	70	12 1/2
CDE	100 sh.	55	50 1/8
DEF	600 sh.	49	5 1/2

Figure 5.13

ADDITIONAL PURCHASE WORKSHEET

Amount Realized from Last Stock Sale $ 7,178

+ Cash Already in Account   0

TOTAL AVAILABLE $ 7,178

STOCKS OWNED (List by points, highest to lowest):

STK. SYMBOL	ORIG. NO. SH.	+ ADD'L SH.	= TOT. SH.	PTS.	CURR. PRICE	AMT. PER 100 SH.*	NO. SH. TO BUY**	AMT. LEFT
ABC	100	0	100	78	82 $\frac{1}{8}$	8,623	—	7,178
BCD	300	0	300	70	12 $\frac{1}{2}$	1,312	300	3,240
CDE	100	0	100	55	50 $\frac{1}{8}$	5,263	—	3,240
DEF	600	0	600	49	5 $\frac{1}{2}$	577	500	490

*Figure current prices times 100, plus 5%.

**Must not be more than "Orig. No. Sh." unless there is only one stock left to buy.

(1) You can't buy ABC, since 100 shares would cost more than $7,178.

(2) You can buy 300 shares of BCD at 12 1/2 for a total cost, with commission, of about $3,938. This leaves you with $7,178 — $3,938 = $3,240.

(3) You can't buy CDE, since 100 shares would cost more than $3,240.

(4) You can buy 500 shares of DEF at 5 1/2 for about $2,750 (you can't buy the entire original number of 600 shares, as it would cost more than $3,240).

(5) The remainder of $3,240 — $2,750 = $490 can be left in your account, to be added in with your next sale proceeds.

b. A few months later our system requires you to sell your 100 shares of CDE, whose price had risen to 57 1/4; the net amount received is $5,439 which, when added to the $490 remaining from the last sale, gives you a total of $5,929. You would also have the amount of any dividends received credited to your account. You might wish to invest that also, but this example assumes that you wish to let your dividends accumulate or withdraw them periodically. Amount available for re-investment: $5,929 (see Figure 5.14):

Stock	Original Purchase	Additional Purchases	Total Purchases	Current Points	Current Price
ABC	100 sh.	-0-	100 sh.	78	89 1/4
BCD	300 sh.	300 sh.	600 sh.	61	15
DEF	600 sh.	500 sh.	1100 sh.	42	8 1/8

(1) You can't buy ABC, since 100 shares would cost more than $5,929.

(2) 300 shares of BCD can be bought. Estimated total cost $4,725, leaving a balance of $1,204.

Figure 5.14

ADDITIONAL PURCHASE WORKSHEET

Amount Realized from Last Stock Sale $ 5,439

+ Cash Already in Account   490

TOTAL AVAILABLE $ 5,929

STOCKS OWNED (List by points, highest to lowest):

STK. SYMBOL	ORIG. NO. SH.	+ ADD'L SH.	= TOT. SH.	PTS.	CURR. PRICE	AMT. PER 100 SH.*	NO. SH. TO BUY**	AMT. LEFT
ABC	100	0	100	78	89 1/4	9,371	—	5,929
BCD	300	300	600	61	15	1,575	300	1,204
DEF	600	500	1100	42	8 1/8	854	100	350

*Figure current prices times 100, plus 5%.

**Must not be more than "Orig. No. Sh." unless there is only one stock left to buy.

(3) You can buy 100 shares of DEF for about $854.

(4) The balance remaining in the account is now $350.

c. The next stock you receive a sell signal on is BCD, at 16 1/2. Your 900 shares brings you a net of $14,108; add the $350 already in the account for a total of $14,458 (see Figure 5.15):

Stock	Original Purchase	Additional Purchases	Total Purchases	Current Points	Current Price
ABC	100 sh.	-0-	100 sh.	74	93 1/2
DEF	600 sh.	600 sh.	1200 sh.	40	10

(1) You can buy 100 shares of ABC for about $9,817, leaving a balance of $4,641.

(2) You can buy 400 shares of DEF for $4,200, leaving $441 in the account.

d. A large corporation has offered to buy DEF for $14 per share. After discussing this offer with your broker, you decide to accept it and tender your shares. You receive $22,400 (there is usually no commission involved in this transaction). Some discount firms will charge a commission on a tender offer; check with the broker to be certain of the firm's policy.
This leaves you with ABC, which by this time is selling at 98 1/2. You own 200 shares and your original purchase was 100 shares. *With only one stock remaining, you may violate the rule of not buying more than the original number of shares purchased.* Your $22,400 plus $441 cash will buy 200 shares, giving you a total of 400 shares, with $2,156 remaining in the account (see Figure 5.16).

Figure 5.15

ADDITIONAL PURCHASE WORKSHEET

Amount Realized from Last Stock Sale $ *14,108*

+ Cash Already in Account   *350*

TOTAL AVAILABLE $ *14,458*

STOCKS OWNED (List by points, highest to lowest):

STK. SYMBOL	ORIG. NO. SH.	+ ADD'L SH.	= TOT. SH.	PTS.	CURR. PRICE	AMT. PER 100 SH.*	NO. SH. TO BUY**	AMT. LEFT
ABC	100	0	100	74	93½	9,877	100	4,641
DEF	600	600	1200	40	10	1050	400	441

*Figure current prices times 100, plus 5%.

**Must not be more than "Orig. No. Sh." unless there is only one stock left to buy.

Figure 5.16

ADDITIONAL PURCHASE WORKSHEET

Amount Realized from Last Stock Sale $ 22,400

+ Cash Already in Account   441

TOTAL AVAILABLE $ 22,841

STOCKS OWNED (List by points, highest to lowest):

STK. SYMBOL	ORIG. NO. SH.	+ ADD'L SH.	= TOT. SH.	PTS.	CURR. PRICE	AMT. PER 100 SH.*	NO. SH. TO BUY**	AMT. LEFT
ABC	100	100	200	74	98½	10,342	200	2,156

*Figure current prices times 100, plus 5%.

**Must not be more than "Orig. No. Sh." unless there is only one stock left to buy.

e. At a later date ABC has risen to 105, but then falls back to 94 1/2, your stop point. You sell your 400 shares for a total of $35,910 which, added to the $2,156, leaves you with $38,066.

f. What do you do now? You take your current issue of the Stock Guide and get to work!

Section G: Summary

1. As soon as you receive your confirmations, prepare:

    a. One Stock Sheet for each of the stocks you bought.

    b. A Summary Sheet that shows all transactions involving receipt or payment of money.

    c. A Dividend Record that shows dividends received, by stock.
        NOTE: If you have sufficient cash accumulated in your account, you may receive interest or dividends from the brokerage house. Enter such amounts in the Dividend Record.

    d. A Weekly Price Chart showing current prices of your stocks and current Stop prices.

2. You must be sure to sell a stock if:

    a. The Weekly Closing Price is at or below the Stop price.

    b. The annual EPS do not show an increase.

    c. The total points are less than 30, or less than 15 if you chose A+ rated stocks.

    d. You receive a tender offer for your shares and accept the offer.

3. After a stock sale, buy additional shares of the remaining stocks in accordance with the example given in Section F.

Conclusion

The system of investment that has been presented in this book is one that should satisfy any type of investor, from the most conservative to the most aggressive.

The system has many advantages, such as:

1. By exclusively selecting companies which grow at a pace that consistently outstrips inflation, your investing in the market should produce results that increase your dollar profits and improve your real wealth.

2. Using stops should protect you from being seriously hurt by any severe, sustained decline in the stock market.

3. The stock selection process gives you an excellent chance of catching stocks that will turn out to be the IBM's of the future and the system of additional purchases should pyramid your holdings in such stocks.

4. Without spending money for advisory services or fees for professional financial planners, you will have the feeling of security that comes from knowing that the stocks you own are among the very best available.

5. You will not be tempted to buy "hot tips" from friends or associates. Tips can be one of the best ways I know to drop a bundle!

Like any system of investing in the market, the real key to success lies in *self-discipline*. If you have the will power to sell when you are supposed to — if you follow all the rules of the system faithfully, you will be well on your way to success!

Appendix

A

Industries

INDUSTRY	CODE NO.	DESCRIPTION
AUTO	21	Manufacturers; auto parts, accessories; rentals; motorcycles
AVIATION	1	Manufacturers of aircraft and parts
BANKS	13	Commercial and savings banks; investment banking; brokerage firms; mortgages; S & L
BREWERS	20	Distillers; beer and whiskey distributors; soft drinks
BUSINESS FORMS	37	Business supplies: manufacture and distribution
CHEMICALS	23	Plastics and chemical manufacturers, distributors, fabricators; paints and coatings
COMPUTERS	10	Manufacturers; software; equipment and components; CAD; services; leasors; retail stores
CONSULTANTS	27	Consultants to all industries
COSMETICS	33	Manufacture, distribution
ELECTRIC	35	Electric and electronic products: industrial and retail

INDUSTRY	CODE NO.	DESCRIPTION
DIVERSIFIED	11	Conglomerates
FOOD	9	Supermarkets, restaurants; food services; processors; grain and meat growers and processors
GLASS	36	Manufacture and marketing
HEALTH CARE	2	Facilities; products; drugs/ pharmaceuticals; hospitals and hospital equipment
HOME PRODUCTS	15	Home builders; interior furnishings; building materials; hardware; carpets
INSTRUMENTS	19	Controls and instruments: manufacture and distribution
INSURANCE	4	Life, casualty and general
MANUFACTURING	32	Heavy equipment; microwave products; machine tools; plant maintenance
METALS	25	Mineral and metal mining and distribution; specialty and precious metals
PAPER	3	Lumber; paper products; publishing and printing; wood products, containers; packaging
PERSONNEL	6	Temporary services; schools and education
PETROLEUM	31	Oil and gas; petroleum products; pipelines; oil drilling and drilling equipment
RECREATION	30	Recreational and leisure products; entertainment; cruise ships; art; gambling; radio and TV; movies; hotels and motels
RETAIL	26	Department stores; discount chains; manufacture and distribution of apparel, jewelry, shoes; catalog sales; toys
RUBBER	28	Rubber products; tires and re-treads; silicon
SECURITY	34	Manufacture and distribution of fire and security products; security systems

INDUSTRY	CODE NO.	DESCRIPTION
TELEPHONE	18	Telephone and telecommuni-cation service and equipment
TRANSPORTATION	24	Trucking; air freight; steam-ship lines; ship-building and repair
UTILITIES	46	Electric and natural gas utili-ties; water-works; nuclear
WASTE MANAGEMENT	12	Services; equipment; asbestos removal
OTHER	48	Cannot be fitted into any of the above categories

Appendix

"Back To School"

Unless you want to take many more hours than necessary, a small calculator is essential in figuring percentages and other calculations that must be made. For those
of you who might not recall your ninth grade arithmetic,
the following information should be useful:

FRACTION =	DECIMAL	FRACTION =	DECIMAL
1/16	.0625	9/16	.5625
2/16 or 1/8	.125	10/16 or 5/8	.625
3/16	.1875	11/16	.6875
4/16 or 1/4	.25	12/16 or 3/4	.75
5/16	.3125	13/16	.8125
6/16 or 3/8	.375	14/16 or 7/8	.875
7/16	.4375	15/16	.9375
8/16 or 1/2	.50		

The quickest way to figure your stops is as follows:

Multiply the price by the reciprocal of the percentage.
The reciprocal is figured by subtracting the percentage
from 100. For example, a stock is bought at 25 3/8. The
Stop table in Chapter 5, Section D, shows you must sell if
the weekly closing price drops by 20%.

1. Figure the reciprocal of 20%:
    100% - 20% = 80%, or .80.

2. Convert 25 3/8 to a decimal by the above chart:
    25 3/8 = 25.375

3. Multiply 25.375 x .80 = 20.30

4. For stocks whose price is quoted in sixteenths
    (usually those whose price is under 5), convert to
    the nearest fraction of 1/16 below; for stocks
    selling above $5, convert to the nearest fraction
    of 1/8 below (see above chart):
    20.30 = 20 1/4

NOTE: If the result in Step 3 above comes out to an
even fraction, such as 20.375 (20 3/8), use that figure as
your stop.

Appendix

C

Operation Of "Winners Only" System

Now that you have read "Winners Only" and understand the explanations of how the system works, you are prepared to follow the system.

The information presented in this Appendix is the heart of the system, without explanations or illustrations. It will enable you to follow the system without having to search constantly throughout the book to see how to proceed.

I. Stock Selection

    A. All stocks, Semi-Final Selection.

        1. Go through the Statistical Section of the S & P Stock Guide. Eliminate by scanning features in the order given below. Proceed to the next line as soon as a stock fails to qualify by any of these features:

    a.   Stock is not a common stock.

    b.   It is a foreign stock that pays in ADR.

    c.   The P/E Ratio is more than twice that of the Dow Jones Industrial Average.

    d.   Current assets do not exceed current liabilities by at least 25%.

    e.   There is preferred stock outstanding exceeding 10% of the shares of common stock.

    f.   Annual EPS have failed to (1) increase each year, or (2) have not doubled in four years, or (3) have not doubled in three years if Year No. 1 shows a deficit.

    g.   6-month or 9-month interim earnings show a decrease.

2. If a stock qualifies by the above factors, put a dash next to it.

3. List the stocks alphabetically that have been marked with a dash. Use a form as shown in Figure 3.2, page 28.

4. Compute the points for all stocks listed and enter under "Total Points". In figuring the points, use a Point Score Work Sheet (Figure 3.5, page 42). Award points as follows:

    a.   S & P Rating: Total Possible Points = 5

IF RATING IS:	POINTS
D	0
C	0.8
B-	1.5
B	2.2
B+ or NR	2.9
A-	3.6
A	4.3
A+	5.0

b. P/E Ratio: Total Possible Points = 25

IF P/E IS:	POINTS	IF P/E IS:	POINTS
Over 21	0	12	12.0
21	.5	11	13.5
20	1.0	10	15.0
19	1.5	9	16.5
18	3.0	8	18.0
17	4.5	7	19.5
16	6.0	6	21.0
15	7.5	5	22.5
14	9.0	4	24.0
13	10.5	3 or less	25.0

c. P/E Ratio as a % of WAG: Total Possible Points = 15
To figure, divide the P/E ratio by the WAG.

%	POINTS
Over 40%	0
35.1 to 40	2.5
30.1 to 35	5.0
27.5 to 30	7.5
22.5 to 27.4	10.0
Under 22.5	15.0

d. Yield: Total Possible Points = 10

% DIVIDEND	POINTS
0 to .4	0
.5 to .9	2
1.0 to 2.0	4
2.1 to 3.0	6
3.1 to 4.0	8
4.1 & over	10

e. Weighted Average Growth (WAG): Total
    Possible Points = 45

IF THE WAG IS:			POINTS
65	or	less	5
65.1	to	74	10
74.1	to	89	15
89.1	to	98	20
98.1	to	107	25
107.1	to	115	30
115.1	to	123	35
123.1	to	131	40
131.1	&	over	45

5. List the top 20% and ties of the point scores on
    a form as shown in Figure 3.3, page 32.

B. Final Selection.

1. Decide on the amount to be invested.

2. Choose the number of stocks according to
    this table:

Amount You Plan To Invest		Eliminate Down To	Number Of
From	To	This Many Stocks	Stocks To Buy
$10,000	$14,999	9	5
15,000	19,999	10	6
20,000	24,999	11	7
25,000	29,999	12	8
30,000	34,999	13	9
35,000	39,999	14	10
40,000	44,999	15	11
45,000	59,999	16	12
60,000	79,999	17	13
80,000	100,000	18	14

For each $25,000 invested over $100,000, add one
stock to each column.

3. In making your choices, use this diversifica-
    tion table:

No. Stocks Bought	Maximum in Same Industry
5 to 7	1
8 to 10	2
11 to 14	3
15 or more	4

C. Stock Selection for the Ultra-Conservative Investor.

Use one of the following methods:

1. Purchase only A+ rated stocks.
   a. Eliminate from consideration all stocks except those with an S & P rating of A+.
   b. Continue the selection process in A above.
   c. Decide on the amount to be invested.
   d. Choose the number of stocks according to this table:

Amount You Plan To Invest		Eliminate Down To	Number Of
From	To	This Many Stocks	Stocks To Buy
$10,000	$19,999	5	3
20,000	29,999	6	4
30,000	39,999	7	5
40,000	59,999	8	6
60,000	79,999	9	7
80,000	100,000	10	8

Each $25,000 over $100,000, add one stock to each column.

   e. In making you choices, use this Diversification Table:

No. Stock Bought	Maximum in Same Industry
3 to 4	1
5 to 6	2
7 to 8	3
9 or more	4

2. Use a Combination System.

Invest a minimum of $20,000 as follows:
   a. Invest a portion of you total investment (minimum $10,000) exactly as described in Chapter 3. Allow the brokerage firm to hold these stocks in street name.

  b. Invest the remaining portion (minimum $10,000) in A+ rated stocks. Take delivery of the stock certificates. Do not sell these stocks unless the S & P rating falls below A+.

II. Stock Purchasing

 A. Have your broker check the stocks you plan to buy. Check the current price and news.

 B. If there is news about any of these stocks that makes them fail to qualify for purchase, substitute from the four reserve stocks.

 C. Place your buy orders "at the market" in round lots. If there is a large spread between the bid and asked price, compute how much over the bid price you can afford to pay. Use this formula:

$$A:B = X:C$$

A = Price at which you computed the Point Score of the stock

B = Point Score of lowest stock that qualifies for purchase

C = Point Score of stock you wish to purchase

X = Highest price per share that you can pay

As far as possible, invest an approximately equal dollar amount in each stock.

III. Record Keeping

 A. Prepare a Stock Sheet for each stock you purchased. See Figure 5.1, page 50.

 B. Prepare a Summary Sheet. See Figure 5.2, page 52.

 C. Using your monthly brokerage statement, make entries of dividends received (by company) on the Dividend Record. Transfer the total figure of dividends received for the month to the Summary Sheet. See Figure 5.3, page 54.

D. Prepare the Weekly Price Chart (Figure 5.4, page 55). Enter the original Stop price in pencil, using this table to figure the Stop Point:

PURCHASE PRICE (OR WEEKLY CLOSE, IF HIGHER)	SELL IF PRICE DROPS:
Under 5	40%
5 1/8 to 10	30%
10 1/8 to 20	25%
20 1/8 to 35	20%
35 1/8 to 70	15%
Over 70	10%

As the weekly closing price hits new highs, re-figure the stop according to the Stop Table above. Erase the previous stop and enter the new stop.
If the stop price is hit on a week when the stock is ex-dividend, add in the amount of the dividend and don't sell if this raises the price above the stop point. But, sell the following week if the price is at or below the stop price. Re-figure the stop if an additional purchase of a stock is made. Use the average cost after the additional purchase.

E. Even if the stop price is not reached, sell the stock if:

1. New annual earnings do not show an increase.

2. After recording new earnings, re-figure the points. If you have selected stocks by I A above, sell if total points are less than 30. If you selected stocks by I B above (A+ rated stocks), sell if total points are less than 15.

3. You receive a buy-out offer and decide to accept it.

IV. Additional Purchases

After selling a stock, prepare an "Additional Purchase Work Sheet" (Figure 5.13, page 70) as follows:

A. List remaining stocks in order of Point Score, highest to lowest.

B. Buy as many shares (in round lots) as you can, up to the original number of shares you purchased.

C. Leave any remaining amount in your account. Add this to the amount received on your next sale.

D. When there is only one stock remaining, buy as many shares, in round lots, as you can.

Glossary

ADR   The abbreviation for American Depository Receipt. A negotiable receipt for shares of a foreign corporation held in the vault of a United States bank. It entitles the owner to all dividends and capital gains. ADR's enable a U.S. citizen to purchase shares of a foreign corporation without trading in overseas markets. For example: A U.S. investor can invest in Benguet Corporation, a Philippine gold mining and engineering company, by purchasing its ADR's which are traded on the New York Stock Exchange.

ACCOUNTANT'S OR AUDITOR'S OPTION   Report by the independent accountants to the Board of Directors and shareholders describing the scope of the examination of the organization's books. It generally states that the audit examination was made in accordance with generally accepted auditing standards...and such other auditing procedures considered necessary in the circumstances.

In the case of a clean audit, the report will further state, "In our opinion, the aforementioned consolidated financial statements present fairly the consolidated financial position of XXX, Inc. and its subsidiaries at December 31, 1989 and 1990.... in conformity with generally accepted accounting principles applied on a consistent basis."

Depending on the audit findings, the opinion can be unqualified or qualified to specific items. Any qualified opinion bears further investigation. The words "subject to" generally mean trouble. Remember that the company's annual report may signal that the company may be on the verge of very serious financial or operating difficulties.

ACCRUED INTEREST   The portion of interest accumulated since the last interest payment. If an investor purchases a bond between interest payment dates, the settlement amount will include the purchase (market) price of the bond plus the amount of interest accrued or accumulated since the last interest payment.

Accrued interest is usually calculated as follows: coupon rate of interest times the number of days since the last payment date.

ACCUMULATED DIVIDEND   The amount of dividends due but not paid. Accumulated dividends on cumulative preferred stock must be paid in full before common stock dividends can be paid.

ACCUMULATION AREA   The price range technicians believe is optimum for purchases of a particular stock. Generally, a stock will not fall below a particular price, providing buying opportunities. A stock's accumulation area may change over time.

ACID-TEST RATIO   The acid-test ratio or quick ratio is used to measure corporate liquidity. It is regarded as an improvement over the current ratio which includes inventory, usually not very liquid.

The acid-test formula is stated as current assets less inventory divided by current liabilities.

ACTIVE MARKET   Reference to the market for a particular stock or the overall market characterized by frequent transactions, narrow bid-offer spreads, and relatively high volume. Active markets can absorb large trades more efficiently. Having a feel for the market can help the investor take advantage of the market's efficiencies. A market order in the active market will most likely be executed at a price near the latest quote. However, in a quiet market, an investor might be in for a rude awakening when placing a market buy order and the price jumps substantially due to a lack of sellers.

ADVANCE-DECLINE LINE The ratio of advancing stocks and declining stocks charted by investors to determine the overall trend of the market. A ratio greater than 1 is bullish and less than 1 is bearish. The steepness of the advance-decline indicates the degree of bullish/bearish sentiment.

AFTER TAX BASIS The comparison of yields on tax-free government bonds and taxable corporate bonds. For example, for a person in the 28% tax bracket, he or she should have to earn 10 percent on a taxable corporate bond investment to match the return on a 7.2% tax-free government bond.

AGAINST THE BOX The box in a short sale is the safe deposit box or account of the short seller. In effect, the investor actually owns the security but makes delivery of the short sale by borrowing stock rather than delivering the owned securities.

Reasons for selling short against the box include: tax strategy to get the benefit of long term capital gains (no longer applicable under recent tax law changes), a desire not to disclose ownership, and inability to deliver the owned shares in the required transaction period.

ALL OR NONE An order by an investor to buy or sell a specified number of units of a security. This prevents the execution of a transaction for only a portion of the securities and eliminates the possibility of paying several commission charges to obtain or sell the specified number of securities.

AMERICAN DEPOSITORY RECEIPT See *ADR*.

ANALYST   A person who studies companies and industries in order to make investment buy and sell recommendations. Most analysts work for brokerage firms, bank trust departments, and mutual funds.

ANNUAL BASIS   The analytical technique of extrapolating annual performance from data covering periods of less than one year.

ANNUAL REPORT   The yearly report issued to stockholders. The SEC requires the company to present an accurate portrayal of events that materially affected operations during the past fiscal year. The report includes a balance sheet, income statement, a description of company operations, and management's discussion of the company and its results.

 The annual report provides a wealth of information. Look for discussion of products, pricing, inventory write-downs, acquisitions, divestitures, long-term debt, and working capital. A more detailed report with the SEC and available from the corporate secretary is the 10k for the full year and 10q for quarterly reporting.

ANNUITY   An investment contract sold by life insurance companies based on a guarantee of fixed or variable payments for a specified period of time beginning in the future, usually tied to retirement. A fixed annuity will pay out an amount in regular installments. A variable annuity payout will vary with the value of the account. The tax-deferred status of the capital and investment proceeds is a prime investment factor. Recent changes in the tax law make annuities an attractive investment alternative.

ARBITRAGE   The act of benefiting from differences in price of the same commodity, currency, or security traded on two or more markets. The arbitrageur makes money by taking advantage of the price disparity by selling in one market while simultaneously buying in another market. Since the disparity is usually very small, a large volume is required to lock in a significant profit for the arbitrageur.

ASCENDING TOPS   A security's chart pattern exhibiting a series of peaks, each higher than the previous peak. Considered bullish, indicating a continuation of rising prices. See *Descending Tops.*

ASKED PRICE   The lowest price a dealer or seller is willing to accept. Also called the offering price. BID is the highest price a dealer or buyer is willing to offer. The difference between bid and asked is called the price spread.

ASSET ALLOCATION   Investment technique based on diversifying the portfolio among different types of assets such as stocks, bonds, cash equivalents, precious metals, real estate, and collectibles. See *Diversification.*

ASSET MANAGEMENT ACCOUNT   A one stop account with a bank, brokerage house or savings institution that offers a combination of services such as check writing, money market funds, credit cards, margin loans and other security transactions. All activity is summarized on one monthly statement.

ASSET PLAY   A stock investment that value investors find attractive because the value of the firm's assets are not properly reflected in its stock price.

AT THE CLOSE   A customer market order to be executed within the last 30 seconds of trading on the exchange. There is no guarantee the order will be executed.

AT THE MARKET   An instruction to buy or sell a security as soon as possible at the best available price.

AT THE MONEY   An option whose exercise or strike price is the same as the current market price of the underlying security.

AT THE OPENING   An instruction to a broker to buy or sell a security at the price that applies when the exchange opens. If the order cannot be executed at that time, it is automatically canceled.

AUTHORIZED SHARES   The maximum number of shares a company can legally create under its articles of incorporation ration. The number of authorized shares can be increased by action of the firm's Board of Directors.

AVERAGE DOWN, AVERAGE UP   Strategies used to purchase stocks over a period of time. To average down, an investor will make an initial purchase at a set price but will wait for downside movement before adding to the stock position. To average up, an investor will purchase equal quantities of the same security as the price rises thus lowering the overall average cost below the current market price.

AWAY FROM THE MARKET   An order that cannot be currently executed because it contains a limit bid, or a limited offer, above prevailing quotes for the security. This strategy is profitable in thinly traded securities where a market order can trigger your sale or purchase.

B

BACK-END LOAD   A charge paid at redemption of a mutual fund or annuity. Usually designed to discourage the withdrawal of funds from an investment. See *Front-End Load*.

BALANCED MUTUAL FUND   A mutual fund that attempts to earn an acceptable return consistent with the low-risk strategy of investing in a mixed portfolio of common stocks, preferred stocks, and bonds. Usually a balanced fund out performs a pure equity fund when stocks are falling and lags pure equity funds in a rising market.

BANKRUPTCY   The insolvency of an individual or organization. A Chapter 7 bankruptcy allows the court to appoint a trustee empowered to make management changes, secure financing, and otherwise operate the business. A Chapter 11 bankruptcy allows the debtor organization protection from creditors while attempting to reorganize the business. Restructuring of debt, labor renegotiation, and new business relationships and terms with suppliers and customers normally occur during this restructuring.

BASIS   The original cost of an investment including all acquisition costs such as commissions. In commodities, the difference between the price of the item being hedged and the price of the futures contract.

BASIS POINT   The measure used to determine movement in bond yield. A basis point equals 0.01% yield. A bond whose yield has increased from 9.25% to 11.05% had a increase of 180 basis points.

BASIS PRICE   The cost of an investment used to determine capital gains or losses.

BEAR   An investor who believes that stock prices will decline either for the market in general or for a particular security. An active bear will sell stocks short, purchase puts, or sell an uncovered call to capitalize on the anticipated decline.

BEAR MARKET   A stretch of time from several months to several years during which stock prices tumble.

BEARER SECURITY   A security payable to the person possessing it. Coupon bonds were bearer bonds in that the clipped coupons could be redeemed by anyone. Most securities are now registered in the name of the owner and can be transferred only upon proper endorsement.

BELLWETHER   A security that takes a leadership position in the direction of the stock market in general or for a particular industry. The phrase, " As General Motors goes, so goes the nation," was predicated on its bellwether position in regard to the national economy.

BETA   A measure of the price volatility of a specific stock in relation to the market in general. The S&P Composite Stock Index has a beta of 1. A more volatile stock would have a beta greater than 1 and would rise and decline faster than the S&P 500. Generally, stocks with betas greater than 1 are more risky while stocks with betas less than 1 have more conservative followings.

BID PRICE   The highest price at which a dealer or buyer is willing to pay for a security. The Asked Price is the lowest price at which a dealer or seller is willing to accept. The difference between bid and asked is called the price spread.

BLIND POOL   A limited partnership that does not disclose the investments the general partner intends to pursue. In contrast, a specified real estate pool, lists the properties acquired, prices paid, and rental income. Blind pools may be used to acquire real estate, high-tech companies, and to fund research and development.

BLOCK TRADING   The purchase or sale of large quantities of stock. Typically, trades involving 10,000 or more shares and $200,000 in value are considered block trades.

BLUE CHIP   Stocks of the highest quality with a long record of earnings and dividend growth. Usually well-known industry leaders known for quality management.

BOND   A long-term debt security obligating the issuer to pay interest and repay the principal. Both corporations and governments issue bonds. The holder holds rights to receive interest and return of principal but has no ownership rights in the issuing corporation.

A convertible bond is exchangeable for corporate stock at a predetermined conversion factor. Therefore, a convertible bond will more closely follow the price actions of the company's common stock.

A secured bond is backed by collateral (corporate assets) while an unsecured bond is backed by the faith and credit of the issuer. In the event of bankruptcy, bondholders have precedent over stockholders. Some bond issues may be subordinate to others so make sure you know the status of your bond holdings in the case of a bankruptcy.

BOND RATING The credit worthiness of a bond issuer as determined by one of several rating services. Moody's Investors Service, Standard and Poor's Corporation, and Fitch Investor's Service, Inc. evaluate bond issuers' financial strength and cash flow with respect to projected interest payments and principal repayment. Ratings range from AAA or Aaa (highest) to D (in default). Bonds rated below B are not investment grade and are termed "junk bonds" in the trade.

BOND RATIO The measure of a corporation's leverage relating bonds as a percentage of total capitalization. The bond ratio is determined by dividing all bonds due after one year by the total of those bonds plus stockholders' equity. Different industries have different normal bond ratios.

Utilities, for instance, have a high bond ratio. Compare the bond ratio of stocks you hold with other companies in the same industry to determine if the company may be over-leveraged. See *Capitalization Ratio* and *Debit-to-equity Ratio*.

BOOK VALUE The value of a particular asset or the value of the company as carried on the accounting records of the business. Company book value is determined by reducing the value of the assets by the intangibles and then deducting all liabilities. Since book value may not approximate real market value, book value per share analysis is a crude method utilized in seeking out under-valued stocks.

BOTTOM The lowest price of a security, commodity, or the market in general for a specified period of time.

Also considered a support level beyond which the price of a security or the market has failed to penetrate after reaching the price range several times. Market technicians chart stock fluctuations seeking bottoms to aid in timing of stock purchases.

BOTTOM UP INVESTING   Investment strategy concentrating on individual stock fundamentals before looking at the big picture implications of different economic scenarios.

BREAK   A significant and rapid drop in price of a security or the market in general.

BREAKOUT   The action of a security or market rising above a resistance level or dropping below a support level thereby breaking the previous trading pattern.

BULL   An investor who believes that stock prices will rise for the market in general or for a particular security. An active bull will purchase shares outright or purchase calls to capitalize on the anticipated advance. See also *Bear*.

BULL MARKET   A stretch of time, from several months to years, in which stock prices rise.

C

CALLS   The provision allowing a bond or preferred stock issuer to recall the issue before maturity (if applicable). The call provision specifies the earliest the issue can be called and spells out other terms and conditions. When purchasing bonds which have appreciated substantially over the maturity value, investigate the call provision in order to avoid having the bond called at less than current market value.

Issuers will recall securities when it is advantageous to retire older issues with higher interest rates than current financing options.

CALL OPTION   A contract giving the holder the right to buy the underlying security at a specific price during a specified period of time. The exercise price of the option is called the "striking price."

CAPITALIZATION RATIO The breakdown of a company's long-term financing showing what percentage is common stock, preferred stock and bonds. The analysis reflects the amount of leverage used by the company. See *Bond Ratio* and *Debt-to-equity Ratio.*

CASH EQUIVALENT Fund asset type containing short-term, liquid investments having a maturity of less than one year. Usually used for temporary investment purposes pending an investment or distribution. Money market accounts at brokerages are denominated in cash equivalents.

CASH FLOW The flow of funds in and out of an operating business. Normally calculated as net income plus depreciation and other non-cash items.

Cash flow analysis is an excellent investment tool in determining the company's ability to meet upcoming cash obligations and as an evaluation tool to ferret out undervalued companies.

CASH RATIO The cash ratio is used to measure liquidity. It is calculated as the sum of cash and marketable securities divided by current liabilities. It indicates how a company can meet current creditor claims.

CHARTING A technical analysis technique used in tracking price trends in order to determine patterns in price movements. A person who charts stocks is termed a chartist in the trade.

CIRCUIT BREAKER Market control techniques enacted by stock and commodity exchanges to restore order to the market by temporarily halting trading when the market has dropped by a specific amount during a specific period of time. Pressure for circuit breakers came in the wake of the October 1987 and October 1989 precipitous market drops.

CLOSE The period just prior to the termination of a trading day at which orders can be filled within the closing price range. Also the final trade of a security for the day.

CLOSED-END FUND   An investment fund with a limited number of shares outstanding. Closed-end funds are usually traded on listed exchanges or over-the-counter.

COMMODITY FUTURE   A commodity contract that obligates the holder to buy or sell a designated unit measure of a commodity at a predetermined price by a specified settlement date.

COMMON STOCK   Class of corporate ownership usually entitled to vote for the Board of Directors and other issues of importance. The Board can vote cash and stock dividends. Preferred stockholders, bond holders, and creditors hold prior claim to corporate assets in the event of a bankruptcy or liquidation

COMMON STOCK EQUIVALENT   Securities that may be exchanged for common stock. In some cases, additional cash must also be exchanged. Common stock equivalents include convertible preferred stock, convertivle bonds, rights and warrants. Common stock equivalents are used in computing the diluted earnings per share. See *Dilution.*

COMMON STOCK RATIO   The relationship of common stock to the total capitalization of the company. It is calculated by dividing the sum of common stock, paid-in surplus and retained earnings by the total capitalization.

CONTINGENT LIABILITIES   Potential obligations that materialize only if certain events occur in the future. Contingent liabilities can arise from pending lawsuits, disputed claims, cases under appeal, possible tax assessments, discounted notes receivable, and contract disputes. For instance, government contractors can have their contract payments reduced if profits exceed federal government limits.

Contingent liabilities should be disclosed in the financial statements or accompanying footnotes. When evaluating a company for investment, be sure to read the footnotes; they contain a wealth of information.

CURRENCY FUTURES Contracts for future delivery of a specified unit of foreign currency at a fixed price in U.S. dollars at a specified date.

CURRENT RATIO A liquidity ratio calculated by dividing current assets by current liabilities.

CURRENT YIELD The effective interest rate based on the annual interest earned divided by the current market price of the bond. For example, a $1,000 bond selling for $850 and paying $80 a year interest has a current yield or 9.41% (80/850). The coupon rate in this example is 8% (80/1,000). See *Yield*.

CUSTOMER'S LOAN CONSENT Agreement between a brokerage firm and margin customer allowing the broker to borrow margined securities (up to the debit balance of the customer) for use in delivery against short sales by other customers or in the event of certain failed deliveries.

CYCLICAL Industries and stocks that tend to follow the fortunes of the economy. When the economy prospers, these industries and stocks tend to rebound and vice versa. The automotive and steel industries and stocks are considered cyclical. Shrewd and patient investors pick up these stocks at attractive prices when the economy is experiencing a trough only to unload them later after late-comers bid up their prices.

D

DAILY TRADE LIMIT On commodity and option markets, the maximum amount a contract is allowed to rise or fall in one day.

DATE OF RECORD The effective date that determines which shareholder officially owns the stock and is thus eligible to receive the cash or stock dividend.

DAY ORDER   A market order to buy or sell securities that expires if not executed before the end of the trading day in which it is entered.

DEBENTURE   A debt instrument backed only by the full faith and credit of the issuing company. Examples include unsecured bonds and commercial paper.

DEBT-TO-EQUITY RATIO   The relationship of a company's total debt to total shareholders' equity as a measure of leverage. It can be used to estimate the vulnerability of future earnings to variation.

DEEP DISCOUNT BOND   A bond originally issued at a par value of $1,000 and now trading at less than 80% (20% discount) of par value.

DEFENSIVE SECURITIES OR INDUSTRIES   Corporate securities and industries that are characterized as being least affected by recessions and general economic downturns. Some defensive industries include food, utility, and other required services or products.

DELAYED OPENING   The postponed trading in a stock due to a large imbalance in buy and sell orders, usually due to a takeover or other substantial event.

DEPOSITORY RECEIPT   See ADR (American Depository Receipt).

DESCENDING TOPS   A security's chart pattern exhibiting a series of peaks, each lower than the previous peak. Considered bearish, indicating a continuation of declining prices. See *Ascending Tops*.

DIFFERENTIAL   The excess charged by dealers for processing "odd lot" transactions. An odd lot is less than 100 share multiples for stocks and less than $1,000 for bonds.

DILUTION The calculation of earnings per share taking into account all convertible securities and common stock equivalents. See also *Common Stock Equivalent* .

DIP A temporary drop in security prices during a sustained market rally. Astute investors follow individual stock trading and price patterns to take advantage of price dips.

DISCLOSURE Corporate information release required by the Securities and Exchange Commission and the appropriate stock exchange. The information may be either positive or negative or have no material effect. For instance: Disclosure of insider sales of company stock may be for personal reasons such as needing money to send a child to college or it may signal lackluster future earnings for the company.

DISCOUNT BROKER A brokerage house that charges substantially lower commissions for executing orders to buy and sell securities. Many discount brokers set up business after "May Day" (May 1, 1975) when the Securities and Exchange Commission ended fixed commissions. Today many banks and other financial institutions also offer discount brokerage services.

DISCRETIONARY ACCOUNT An account authorizing the broker to execute security transactions without providing the client with prior information on the trade to be executed. Unless an investor has complete faith in the broker and the broker's investment judgment, discretionary accounts can lead to disagreements not to mention disappointing investment returns.

DIVERSIFICATION The spreading of investment risk by owning different types of securities, precious metals, and money market funds. Stocks are spread between different companies across several industries. See *Asset Allocation.*

DIVIDEND   A distribution of profits to shareholders. Dividends are usually paid quarterly at a set rate which is reviewed periodically by the Board.

DIVIDEND PAYOUT RATIO   The percent of current earnings paid out to stockholders in cash dividends. See *Yield*.

DIVIDEND REINVESTMENT PLAN   Investment offered by many companies allowing shareholders to reinvest their dividends in more shares of the company stock. Usually brokerage fees are absorbed by the company and some also discount the stock price.

E

EARNINGS PER SHARE   Net after tax income of a corporation applicable to each share of common stock. If there are outstanding convertible securities, the unadjusted earnings per share are called primary earnings. Earnings per share adjusted to account for convertible securities are called fully diluted earnings.

ECONOMIC INDICATORS   Economic statistics reflecting the general direction of the economy. Some indicators are termed leading indicators because they tend to lead or forecast the direction of the economy or business cycle. The stock market is known as a leading indicator.

Other examples of economic indicators include: Utility usage, unemployment rate, balance of trade, interest rates, inventory changes, and building permits.

EFFECTIVE RATE   The yield on a debt security based on its purchase price. The effective rate and the coupon rate may vary substantially depending on the price of the debt security, which takes into account current interest rates and changes in the company's financial position since issuance of the debt security.

EFFICIENT MARKET A market which takes into account all known information quickly and accurately. Efficient market advocates consider all information automatically reflected in the price of a security; therefore, it is impossible to "discover" undervalued companies.

EQUITY A security possessing ownership interests in a corporation. Usually called stock.

EQUIVALENT BOND YIELD The measurement or yield on U.S. Treasury bills on an annualized basis if held to maturity.

EX-DIVIDEND The date on which the purchaser of a stock does not receive the dividend. Any purchase of the stock on that date or after will be ex-dividend. Usually the opening price of the stock will be reduced by the value of the dividend.

F

FILL The execution of an order to purchase or sell a security.

FILL OR KILL A limit order to purchase or sell a security that instructs the broker to cancel the order if it cannot be executed immediately. Fill or kill orders are generally entered for large trades which may trigger a significant price change if not executed immediately.

FILTER RULE A technical trading rule specifying a breakpoint for an individual stock or market average. Trades are executed when the price change is greater than the filter.

FINANCIAL FUTURE A futures contract on interest-sensitive securities or financial assets. Examples include Treasury bonds, certificates of deposit, stock indexes, and currencies.

FIRST CALL DATE   The earliest date at which the issuer can call a debt security for redemption. The bond indenture will spell out all call dates, call prices, and applicable call terms and conditions.

FISCAL YEAR   The twelve month accounting period for determining the profit or loss for an entity. The fiscal year may or may not correspond to the regular calendar year. Many companies maintain fiscal years different from calendar years due to the physical nature or business cycle of their industry.

FIXED ANNUITY   Investment contract sold by insurance companies which guarantees fixed payments for life or for a specified period. In contrast, a variable annuity's payments vary depending on the underlying portfolio. See *Variable Annuity* and *Annuity*.

FIXED-CHARGED COVERAGE   Analysis of a corporation's income before interest and taxes to interest on bonds and other long-term debt. Bond rating services use fixed-charge coverage in determining the bond safety and thus its rating.

FIXED-INCOME SECURITY   A security with specific payment dates and amounts. Bonds and preferred stocks are fixed-income securities.

FLAG   Technical analysis chart pattern designating consolidation before a breakout. The chart of price fluctuations in a narrow trading range resembles a flag and is preceded and followed by steep price advances or declines.

FLASH   Delay in market tape more than five minutes due to heavy trading volume. A flash interrupts the tape display to report the current or flash price of a heavily traded security.

FLAT BOND   A bond that trades without accrued interest. Bonds that are in default trade flat. Accrued interest will be paid to the buyer if and when the accrued interest is paid, no interest is paid to the seller of a bond trading flat.

FLAT MARKET Price action of a security or the market in general that exhibits a horizontal price movement due to little or no market activity.

FLOAT The number of shares held by the investing public. Stocks with small float are susceptible to sharp price movements.

FLOOR BROKER A registered member of the exchange who executes buy and sell orders on the floor of the exchange for customers of his member firm.

FLOOR TRADER A registered member of an exchange who trades for his or her private account.

FORCED CONVERSION A conversion instigated by the issuer calling in the security for redemption. A forced conversion generally happens when the underlying stock has risen sharply and the convertible has risen above the call price. The owner of the convertible has a choice of converting, selling the security or accepting the call price which is lower than current market price.

FORMULA INVESTING Investment strategy attempting to limit emotional decision making. Most formula investing strategies are based on timing or price levels. For example, dollar cost averaging and apportioning investment between stocks and bonds depending on stock and bond price relationships.

FORWARD CONTRACT A contract for the delivery of a specified commodity, security, currency or financial instrument at a specified rate at a future specified date.

FOURTH MARKET A computerized communications network linking institutional investors for purposes of executing trades between the institutions without using a brokerage firm.

FRACTIONAL DISCRETION ORDER   A buy or sell order for securities that gives the broker discretion to execute the order within a specified fraction of a point. For example, a fractional discretion order to purchase 500 shares of Benguet Corporation at $6 a share, discretion one-quarter point, means that the broker can execute the order at any price up to and including $6.25 a share. The customer knows up front what the maximum cost will be and does not run the risk of paying too much if the price surges or of missing the purchase if the stock opens at 6 $\frac{1}{4}$ and never reaches $6 a share.

FREDDIE MAC   The nickname for the Federal Home Loan Mortgage Corporation (FHLMC), which establishes and serves as a secondary market for the conventional mortgage market and thrift institutions.

FREE CREDIT BALANCE   Cash in a customer's brokerage account which may be withdrawn by the customer at any time. Funds received in short sales are held in escrow and are not part of the free credit balance.

FRONT-END LOAD   A charge paid upon the initial purchase of a mutual fund or annuity. The investor should consider the return needed to recover this front-end charge and still be an attractive investment. See *Back-end Load.*

FULLY DILUTED EARNINGS PER SHARE   The adjusted earnings per share for common stock after taking into account all convertible securities. When the convertible securities have not been converted, earnings will be reported for both primary earnings and fully diluted earnings per share.

FULL-SERVICE BROKER   A brokerage firm providing total investment and financial services to its customers. Full-service brokers generally work on a commission basis. In contrast to discount brokers, full-service broker fees are higher to cover the cost of investment research and financial advice given the client.

FUNDAMENTAL ANALYSIS The analytical approach to investing that is based on the intrinsic value of the company. The underlying economic value of the company is determined by review of the company's balance sheet and income statements. Fundamental analysis attempts to predict a company's future performance based on the analysis of its fundamental strengths and weaknesses. Analysis of a company's financial ratios, for instance, may signal an under-valued situation.

FUTURES CONTRACT An agreement providing for the future exchange of a financial asset or commodity at an agreed-upon price in a future determined month. A futures contract obligates the seller to sell the underlying financial investment or commodity and the buyer to purchase the underlying financial instrument or commodity at the predetermined price on settlement date. The contract can be sold to another investor to close out the position. Do not confuse options with futures contracts. With an option, the buyer may choose to exercise the option, while a futures buyer is committed to fulfill the futures contract.

FUTURES EXCHANGE A marketplace for the trading of futures contacts in financial instruments or commodities. Certain futures exchanges specialize in different kinds of futures contracts, for example, The Chicago Rice and Cotton Exchange. Other well-known futures exchanges include The Commodity Exchange (Comex), The Chicago Mercantile Exchange, The International Monetary Market, and The New York Futures Exchange.

G

GOLDEN PARACHUTE Provisions passed by the board of directors providing lucrative contracts for key executives. Golden parachutes provide security for executives in the case of an unfriendly takeover. They are now part of poison-pill provisions geared at preventing takeover efforts. The golden parachute provisions may include a bonus, general termination pay package, stock options, and a consulting agreement.

GOOD DELIVERY Delivery of a certificate that has met all the necessary requirements to enable proper transfer of title to the purchasing investor.

GOOD-TILL-CANCELLED ORDER A limit or stop order placed by an investor that instructs the broker that the order shall remain in effect until filled or cancelled by the investor. Some brokerage houses automatically cancel Good-Till Cancelled orders (GTC) after thirty days. In addition, stocks trading under one dollar are usually restricted to Day Orders. GTC orders are very handy for the investor who wants to purchase or sell a stock at a particular price and does not mind waiting for the stock to reach that price level. A GTC order helps insure the investor the stock trade will be executed at the specified price even though he or she cannot actively follow the stock's price on a timely basis.

GRANTOR The term for the options trader who either sells a call or put option and earns premium income. The grantor sells the right to buy a security at a specific price with a call and the right to sell a security at a specific price with a put. See *Premium Income.*

GREENMAIL Payment by a takeover target to prevent an unfriendly takeover, usually involving repurchase of stock for substantially more than the acquiring company paid for the investment position.

GROSS SPREAD The difference between public offering price of a new securities issue and the proceeds received by the issue. The difference is composed of the underwriter's discount, manager's fee and the selling group concession or discount.

GROWTH FUND A mutual fund specializing in growth stocks. Like their growth stock counterparts, growth funds ten to rise more rapidly in bull markets and fall more sharply in bear markets.

GROWTH INVESTMENTS Companies or industries whose earnings are projected to rise substantially above the performance of other companies or industries. A growth stock tends to invest its capital and utilize its assets to realize a rate of return well in excess of its cost of capital.

GUARANTEED BOND Contract issued by insurance companies to pension and profit-sharing plans that guarantees a specific rate of return for the contract life. The retirement plans lock in an acceptable return while the insurance company assumes the investment risks including market movement, interest rate changes, and credit risks for the underlying security portfolio. The insurance company stands to gain if the actual return on investments exceeds the guaranteed rate of return.

H

HEAD AND SHOULDERS A stock or commodity chart pattern outlining the head and shoulders of a person. Technical analysts interpret the pattern as signaling a price trend reversal. As the price pattern forms the right shoulder, technicians view the trend bearish and a forbearer of lower stock prices. In contrast, a reverse head and shoulders stock pattern has the head near the bottom of the chart, indicating a price rise in the future.

HEDGING An investment position utilizing offsetting securities positions to minimize the risk of financial loss.

Examples include a position in a futures market to offset the position held in the cash market, holding security and selling short against the box, and a call option against a shorted stock. A perfect hedge eliminates the possibility for a future gain or loss. An imperfect hedge insures against a portion of the loss. See *Short Against The Box.*

HIGH FLYER A highly-speculative and over-priced stock whose price varies sharply over a short period of time. Usually the result of rumors involving reports of technological breakthroughs in high-technology issues, medical breakthroughs in biotechnology stocks or significant mineral deposit finds in mining stocks.

HIGH-GRADE BOND A bond receiving AAA (Aaa) or AA (Aa2) ratings form the bond rating services.

HIGH-PREMIUM CONVERTIBLE BOND A long-term convertible bond offering an attractive interest rate which commands a premium substantially over the value at which it is convertible into common stock.

HIGH-TECH STOCK Securities of companies in high technology industries such as biotechnology, laser, robotics, fiber-optics, semiconductors, electronics and communication. High-tech stocks generally command higher P/E ratios and exhibit volatile earnings growth and stock price movements.

HISTORIC TRADING RANGES The price range within which a security has traded since going public. Other historical trading ranges include the 52-week range listed in the *Wall Street Journal* and the year's highs and lows as listed in stock guides such as *Standard and Poor's.*

HISTORIC YIELD The yield listed by money market and mutual funds. Usually computed by dividing the annual yield by a reasonable average.

HOLDER OF RECORD The investor whose name is registered as the security owner at the close of business on the recorded date set by the company. Entitlement to cash and stock dividends is determined by the holder of record on that date.

I

IMBALANCE OF ORDERS A significant oversupply of either buy or sell orders in relation to each other. The imbalance may be the result of a major news event affecting the security such as takeover rumors, major mineral find or technological breakthrough, announced stock split or significantly higher or lower earnings results. The over imbalance hampers the orderly market process and trading may be suspended in their stock until sufficient offsetting orders are placed to correct the imbalance.

IMMEDIATE PAYMENT ANNUITY An annuity purchased with a single payment requiring annuity payments to begin immediately. Usually, monthly payments continue for the life of the annuity holder or for a predetermined number of years as elected by the purchaser. See *Annuity*.

INDIVIDUAL RETIREMENT ACCOUNT (IRA) A tax-deferred personal retirement account in which an employed individual and spouse may deposit up to $2,000 a year ($2,250 including a non-working spousal deposit and $4,000 if both persons are working). For a couple filing jointly, the maximum $2,000 deduction for each spouse is phased out if adjusted gross income (AGI) is between $40,000-$50,000. No deduction is allowed if AGI is $50,000 or more. Prior to recent tax changes, all working people were allowed a tax deduction for IRA contributions. Now more stringent eligibility tests must be passed to permit a tax deduction form taxable income.

IRA portfolios may be invested in various financial vehicles: stocks, bonds, certificates of deposit, mutual funds, money market account, etc.

INITIAL MARGIN   The amount of equity which a customer must deposit with a broker prior to making a margin transaction. The broker furnishes the balance, charging margin interest rates. Minimum margin requirements are set by the Federal Reserve Board under Regulation T but many brokerage firms have stricter margin requirements.

IPO (Initial Public Offering) A corporation's first public offering of stock, usually underwritten by a single investment banker or a pool of investment bankers and brokerage firms. Depending on market circumstances and the individual firm's financial expertise, a firm may make its offering directly to the public.

INSIDE INFORMATION   Material information not known by the general public that would influence the price of the affected company's stock. Examples would be takeover information, favorable or unfavorable news relating to company earnings or operations, and dividend or stock split information. SEC regulations forbid persons with inside information to trade in the stock for their personal benefit. The 1980's experienced a substantial increase in insider trading investigations, indictments and convictions.

INSIDE MARKET   Also called the wholesale market, the inside market is where dealer-brokers trade with each other for their own account. Typically, the spread between bid and asked prices in the inside market is smaller than in the outside or retail market.

INSIDER   Anyone having access to material corporate information. Generally used to indicate corporate officers and board of directors. SEC regulations prohibit the trading by those possessing inside information.

INSTITUTIONAL BROKER   A broker who services the security transactions for major investor institutions such as banks, insurance companies, mutual funds, health and welfare and pension funds, and trust institutions.

INSTITUTIONAL INVESTOR Investor organizations that trade large volumes of securities thereby commanding reduced commissions and other special treatment. A substantial portion of daily trading is for the account of institutional investors such as banks, trusts, pension funds, insurance companies, and mutual funds.

INSURED ACCOUNT As related to securities transactions, brokerage accounts are insured by the SIPC (Securities Investor Protection Corporation). Total coverage is $500,000 per account. Cash coverage is limited to $100,000 per account. Some brokerage firms provide additional insurance for their customers backed by blanket bonds.

INTERCOMMODITY SPREAD A commodity trading technique where an investor attempts to profit from the price relationship between related commodities by maintaining a long position in one commodity and a short position in a related commodity.

INTERDELIVERY SPREAD A trading strategy where an investor attempts to profit from the price difference fluctuations by simultaneously purchasing a contract for one month and selling the same contract in another month.

IN THE MONEY An option is said to be in the money if the current market price is higher than the striking price of a call option.

L

LIQUIDITY The ease at which financial assets can be converted to cash without creating a substantial change in price or value. Liquidity is influenced by the amount of float in the security, investor interest, and size of the investment being converted to cash.

LISTED OPTION Put or call options traded on a registered exchange.

LISTED STOCK   Stock or bond securities that have met the listing requirements of the particular stock exchange and are actively traded on that exchange. Typical requirements include demonstrated earning power, asset valuation, broad distribution of stock and minimum market value. Unlisted stocks are traded over-the counter. Generally, listing provides liquidity, an orderly market and price spreads, protective regulations, financial information requirements, and higher collateral value for loan purposes.

Stock exchanges and the SEC have rules for suspension of trading and delisting.

LOAD FUND   Mutual funds with sales charges. Mutual funds without sales charges (load fees) are termed no-load funds.

LOANED FLAT   The loaning of securities to cover short positions without a charge or premium.

LOCKED MARKET   A condition in a highly competitive market when the bid and offer prices for a security are the same. After the offsetting purchases and sales are completed and additional buyers and sellers enter, the market unlocks.

M

M1   The standard measure of money supply comprised of currency, demand deposits and other checkable deposits.

M2   M1 plus savings and small time deposits, money market deposit accounts and shares in money market funds.

M3   M2 plus large time deposits.

MAINTENANCE MARGIN   The minimum equity value that must be maintained in a margin account. Regulation T requires a deposit of $2,000 before any credit can be extended.   Initial margin requirements of 50% of the market value of margined positions must be maintained. Individual brokerage houses generally have tighter margin requirements called house maintenance requirements. When the market value of margined securities drops below the minimum margin percent, a margin call is sent to the customer requesting additional cash or securities as collateral.

MANAGED ACCOUNT   An investment account where the investor has turned over direction of the account to a professional manager.   Investment advisory firms and trust departments handle managed accounts for a management fee, generally a percentage of asset valuation.

MARGIN   The equity an investor deposits with the broker to borrow additional funds to purchase securities. The initial margin is set by regulation. Maintenance margin is the minimum acceptable percentage difference between the underlying security's current market value and the amount borrowed from the broker. The account where margin transactions are carried out is called a margin account.

MARGIN CALL   A demand from the broker for additional cash or securities to bring the margin account back within minimum maintenance limits.

MARGIN AGREEMENT   The written agreement signed by the client that details how the broker loans money or stock to a customer.

MARKET BREADTH   The percentage of stocks involved in a market move. A market move with good breadth signals strength and a longer-lasting move. Market breadth can be monitored by the advance/decline statistics published in major investment publications.

MARKET IF TOUCHED ORDER (MIT)   A transaction order specifying to buy when the commodity reaches the specified price; the MIT order then becomes a market order to be executed at the best possible available price.

MARKET MAKER   The dealer in the over-the-counter market who maintains firm bid and offer prices for a specific security by being willing to buy or sell a round lot of the security. The market maker performs the same functions in the over-the-counter market that a specialist performs on the exchange.

MARKET ORDER   An order specifying to purchase or sell at the best possible price when the order reaches the trading floor. The broker must purchase at the lowest price available or sell at the highest price available immediately.

MARKET PRICE   The last reported sales price on an exchange and the average of bid and asked prices in the over-the-counter market.

MARKET TIMING   An investment strategy based on evaluation of such factors as technical indicators, interest rates, market direction and strength, and other economic factors. The strategy attempts to time purchases and sales of securities to maximize investment return.

MARKET TONE   The health and vitality of the market. Market tone is positive when dealers and market makers trade actively on narrow bid and offer spreads. Market tone is negative when trading spreads widen and trading is inactive.

MARK TO THE MARKET   The process of debiting and crediting gains and losses resulting in changes in market prices of the underlying securities. Mark to the market is used in short sale and margin accounts.

MAY DAY On May 1, 1975, fixed minimum brokerage commissions were ended allowing brokerage firms to set their own commission rate schedules. See *Discount Broker.*

MINUS TICK The sale of a security at a price lower than the previous sale. Also called downtick.

N

NONREFUNDABLE A bond that the issuer is prevented from retiring with the proceeds of a subsequent issue. The nonrefundable provision may be permanent or restricted to refunding at specific future dates or at specific interest rates.

NO-PAR STOCK Stock without face value. The major advantage to a company issuing no-par stock is price flexibility. The issue may be sold at any price and the value for balance sheet purposes may be fixed by the Board of Directors.

NOT HELD (NH) A market offered instruction allowing the floor broker latitude in time and /or price in executing the best possible purchase or sale. The floor broker is not held accountable if the order is not executed at the best terms available.

NR (NOT RATED) Symbol used by ratings services indicating a security has not been rated. There is neither a negative or positive implication by the NR symbol.

O

ODD-BALL THEORIES Investment theories not readily explained by ratings investment behavior or techniques but with proven track records of price movements coincidentally related to events external to the stock market and the investing world.

ODD LOT   Any securities trade made in less than round lot (100 share) multiples. Brokers charge higher commissions for executing odd lot transactions.

ORIGINAL ISSUE DISCOUNT BOND   A bond issue that is offered at a discount from par value by the original underwriter in the primary market. The discount is usually offered to attract investors to bond issues with coupon rates lower than current market rates. Zero coupon bonds are examples of original issue discount bonds that are attractive investments for IRA's.

OUT OF THE MONEY   An option is said to be out of the money if the current market price is lower than the striking price of a call option or higher than the striking price of a put option. An out of the money option may still have some value due to the possibility that the underlying stock price will move prior to expiration of the option. See *Striking Price.*

OVER THE COUNTER (OTC)   A securities market not conducted through a formal exchange. Over-the-counter securities are traded via a telephone and computerized network linking over-the-counter security dealers. The National Association of Securities Dealers (NASD) oversees over-the-counter transactions and regulations.

P

PAR VALUE   The value assigned to a security upon issuance. For bonds and preferred stock, par value is equivalent to face value. Common stock par value is assigned arbitrarily and is of little significance.

PARITY   Situation when the value of the underlying security equals the market value of the convertible security. For example, parity exists if a bond is convertible into 25 shares of common stock and the bond currently sells for $1,000 and the stock sells for $40 a share.

PARTICIPATING PREFERRED STOCK A preferred stock paying a specified dividend but which also shares or participates in any additional earnings distributions to shareholders. Most preferred stocks are non-participating. An example of a participating preferred stock is one with a specified dividend of $2.50 a share but which will share in additional earnings distributions up to $1.00 a share.

PASSED DIVIDEND An anticipated dividend on stock which is not declared by the board of directors. A passed dividend on common shares does not have to be made up by the company. In contrast, a passed dividend on cumulative preferred shares must be accrued and paid before any common stock dividends can be paid.

PAYDOWN The refunding of an outstanding bond issue via the floating of a smaller debt issue. For example, a company can paydown a $50 million outstanding debt issue with a high interest rate of 15% with a smaller bond issue of $40 million yielding 10%.

PAYMENT DATE Date on which a dividend or interest payment will be made in cash.

PAYOUT RATIO A stock performance measurement signifying the percentage of a company's profit paid out as dividends to common shareholders. Typically, growth companies retain earnings to spur further growth, while old line companies, banks, and utilities tend to have higher payout ratios.

PENNANT A stock or commodity stock pattern outlining a pointed flag or pennant facing to the right. The pennant figure forms as the peaks and valleys become less pronounced, usually on reduced trading volume. Like its flag pattern counterpart, pennants are followed by steep price advances or declines. See *Flag*.

PENNY STOCKS Originally stocks selling for less than $1 a share. Inflation has taken its toll and penny stocks now refer to highly speculative stocks selling for up to $10 as share. Most penny stocks are traded over the counter or on smaller regional exchanges. Natural resource firms such as gold mining and oil exploration companies have traditionally used the penny stock market to raise capital. Today, any high-tech computer and biotechnology companies are first issued as penny stocks.

PERFORMANCE FUND   An investment company mutual fund which invests its portfolio in high growth companies paying little or no dividends. The strategy is to share in above-average growth and stock returns rather that depend on dividend yield to earn acceptable earnings.

PERFORMANCE STOCK   Company whose earnings are projected to rise substantially above the performance of the market in general. A performance stock tends to reinvest its capital and earnings in assets to realize an above-average rate of return.

PERIODIC PAYMENT PLAN An investment plan offered by mutual funds requiring regular monthly or quarterly investments. The investor signs a contract specifying periodic payments over a 10-, 15-, or 20-year period. Most plans offer completion insurance and have asset withdrawal privileges over the contract life after completion of the pay-in requirements. Benefits to investors include a diversified portfolio, reinvestment privileges, and dollar cost averaging. See *Dollar Cost Averaging.*

PERPENDICULAR SPREAD   An option investment strategy involving options with the same expiration dates but different strike price.

PINK SHEET STOCKS   Over-the-counter stocks that are not routinely traded or in the NASDAQ listings. They are listed on pink sheets compiled by the National Quotations Bureau daily. The pink sheets contain bid and asked prices and market makers for these highly traded over-the-counter stocks. Thinly traded debt securities are listed on yellow sheets.

PLAN COMPLETION INSURANCE Decreasing term life insurance offered to investors in mutual fund period payment plans. The insurance provides assurance of the plan continuation should the investor die before completing the plan contact. See *Periodic Payment Plan.*

PREMIUM The amount by which the market value of a preferred stock or bond exceeds its face value or par. For options, the premium is the amount paid by the option buyer for the right to purchase or sell a security during a specified time frame.

PREMIUM INCOME The income earned by an investor who sells put or call options. The investor who sells put and call options in order to earn premium income is called a grantor. The investor who writes options on owned underlying stock is said to be writing a covered option. If the underlying stock is not owned, the investor is writing a naked option. See *Grantor.*

PRICE CONTINUITY The situation when prices exhibit a high degree of continuity in a series of transactions. High price continuity provides more liquidity in the event a position has to be sold out.

PRICE/EARNINGS RATIO One of the most frequently used measurements of a stocks' relative value to other stocks and the market in general. The price/earnings ratio (P/E) is determined by dividing the stock's market price by its earnings per common share. The P/E expresses how much an investor is paying for a potential future stream of earnings.

Generally companies with high P/E's are high-tech, relatively young companies in fast growing industries such as biotechnology, electronics, etc.

PROGRAM TRADING Computerized strategy used by institutional investors to effect simultaneous buy and sell transactions triggered by rising or falling prices in order to profit from price discrepancies between an index of stock futures or options and the market price of the underlying stocks.

PROSPECTUS   The printed summary of the registration statement which the SEC requires the issuer to furnish to prospective investors. The prospectus contains material information about the security offering, the company lines of business, financial information, management, litigation, and operations. A preliminary prospectus is called a red herring.

PROXY   The authorization or power of attorney signed by a stockholder assigning the right to vote the shares to another party. The company management mails proxy statements to registered stockholders prior to the annual stockholder's meetings. The statement contains a brief explanation of proposed management sponsored voting items along with the opportunity to vote for or against each individual issue or transfer the right to vote for the issues to company management or another party.

PUT OPTION   A contract giving the holder the right to sell the underlying security at a specific price during a specified period of time. The exercise price of the option is called the "striking price." See *Call Option*.

Q

QUALITATIVE ANALYSIS   Security analaysis that uses subjective judgement in evaluating securities based on finacial infornation such as managment expertise, cyclicality of industry, strength of research and development, and labor relations.

QUANTITATIVE ANALYSIS   Security analysis that uses financial information derived from company balance sheets, income statements, and 10k's to make an informed investment decision. Examples of quantitative analysis include review of company financial ratios, the cost of capital asset valuation, and sales and earnings trends.

QUICK RATIO   The quick ratio or acid-test ratio is used to measure liquidity. It is regarded as an **improvement**

over the current ratio which includes inventory, usually not very liquid.

The quick ratio is stated as current assets less inventory divided by current liabilites. An alternative divides cash, marketable securities and accounts receivable by current liabilities.

Normally, a quick ratio of 1 to 1 is satisfactory.

QUIET PERIOD Period of time when the issue is in registration and the company is precluded from making promotional statments.

QUOTE A quote or quotation is the highest bid and lowest offer available for a security. The difference between the bid and ask is termed the price spread.

R

RANGE The high and low price extremes over which the security has traded over a specific period of time. The *Wall Street Journal, Investor's Daily*, and *Barron's* list the 52-week price range; Standard & Poor's tear sheets list the calendar year range; the company annual reports list fiscal year price ranges.

Analysis of price ranges can help determine price support levels (bottoms) and tops for specific securities in certain time frames. A push through a bottom or top could signal strong downward or upward momentum.

RATING The result of the review of the credit worthiness of a firm. Rating services such as Moody's Fitch, and Standard & Poor's evaluate a firm to determine the credit risk of investing in the firm's securities.

RATIO ANALYSIS A quantitative investment analysis technique used to compare a company relative to other investment opportunities and the market in general. Changes in ratios can help signal important changes in the direction of the company's fortunes. Examples of ratios include price/earnings, acid-test or quick, debt or equity, inventory turnover, and gross margin.

REALIZED YIELD   The return actually earned on a bond as opposed to the yield at maturity.

RECORDED DATE   The date determining who is eligible for dividends issued by the company. A dividend is declared by the Board to holders on the record date. Also called date of record.

REDEMPTION   Repayment of the principal amount of debt security in order to retire the debt. Redemption privileges are spelled out in the bond indenture. Redemption can be made before or at maturity depending upon call privileges. See *Calls*.

RED HERRING   Slang term for a preliminary prospectus derived from the red caveat printed on the cover *See Prospectus*.

REGISTERED SECURITY   A Security registered on the books of the company with the owner's name.   A registered security needs to be properly endorsed before effective title can be transferred. In contrast, a bearer security is owned by the person possessing it. See *Bearer Security*.

REHYPOTHECATION   The repledging of securities which were originally pledged by the investor to the broker to cover purchases of other securities or to cover short sales. Typically, pledge securities act as collateral for margin loans. Upon signing of the margin account agreement, the investor authorizes the broker to repledge or rehypothecate the securities as collateral for a bank loan to finance the customer's margin account.

REINVESTMENT RATE RISK   The interest rate risk resulting from the uncertainty of the rate at which future interest and other investment cash flows can be reinvested.

RELATIVE STRENGTH The technical analysis technique which compares the ratio of a stock's price to a market index or other index. The ratios are plotted over time to form a graph of relative price.

RESIDUAL SECURITY A security with the potential to dilute earnings on common stock. Examples of residual securities include convertible bonds, preferred stock, and rights and warrants. See *Common Stock Equivalent, Dilution, Earnings Per Share, Fully Diluted Earnings and Per Share, and Rights.*

RESISTANCE LEVEL The upper price level at which the stock price has trouble breaking through. As stock prices reach a resistance level stock holders will sell in hopes of repurchasing the shares after the stock price falls from the resistance level. Plotting of stock prices will indicate potential resistance levels. The lower end of the price range is called the support level.

RESTRICTED ACCOUNT A margin account where the actual margin is between the initial margin and the maintenance margin requirement. When an account is restricted, additional margin purchases are prohibited.

RETIREMENT The calling of debt securities or preferred stock. Securities may be retired through early redemption call privileges or through the floating of another security issue. See *Redemption.*

REVERSAL Technical analysis term describing a major shift in direction of an investment security or market index as evidenced by its chart. Reversals must be distinguished from short term price changes resulting form normal market activity. A true reversal signals a major sustained direction change.

REVERSE SPLIT The reduction of the number of shares outstanding accompanied by an increase in the par value of the shares. The total number of shares have the same market value before and after the reverse split. A company would effect a reverse split in order to raise the price at which its shares are trading.

REWARD-TO-VARIABILITY RATIO   A measure of portfolio performance calculated as the ratio of excess portfolio return (return less the risk-free rate) to risk as measured by beta. See *Beta* and *Risk Free Rate Of Return*.

REWARD-TO-VOLATILITY RATIO   A measure of portfolio performance calculated as the ratio of excess portfolio return (return less the risk-free rate) to risk as measured by beta. See *Beta* and *Risk Free Rate of Return*.

RIGHT   A privilege granted by the corporation to existing stockholders allowing them to subscribe to shares of an upcoming issue before it is offered to the general investing public. The current shareholder can purchase new shares in proportion to number of shares currently owned in relation to total outstanding share. A major advantage of rights is that the shares can be purchased at below market price. Rights are short-term options allowing the holder to purchase a specified number of shares from the corporation at a specific subscription price.

The rights, also known as subscription rights, are transferable and may be sold to others. To act on the offer, the shareholder sends the rights and the required dollar amount to the company or his broker for execution. See *Common Stock Equivalents*.

RISK   The financial uncertainty that the actual return of an investment will be different from the expected return. Factors of risk that can affect an investment include inflation or deflation, currency exchange, liquidity, default by borrower, and interest rate fluctuations.

RISK-AVERSE INVESTOR   An investor who will not assume a given level of risk unless there is an expectation of adequate compensation. Investors generally seek investments with the least amount of risk. The greater the risk, the greater the return demanded.

RISK-FREE ASSET An asset with a certain expected rate of return and a zero variance of return.

RISK-FREE RATE OF RETURN The return on a riskless asset. For example, the rate of return on U.S. Treasury securities.

RISK PREMIUM The additional compensation demanded by investors, above their risk-free rate of return, for assuming additional risk. The higher the additional risk, the larger the risk premium.

RISK-SENSITIVE Investor decision-making process designed to reduce the potential for loss or a rate of return less than anticipated.

ROUND LOT The normal trading unit for a security. The size of the round lot can vary depending on the type of security and the price. Moderately priced stocks typically trade in round lots of 100 shares.

ROUND TURN The cycle of opening and closing out a futures position. Commodity brokerage commissions are based on a round turn.

S

SALES CHARGE The fee charged by an investment company, mutual fund, or unit investment trust when shares or units are purchased. Generally the fee is a percentage of the dollar value of the purchase. Funds without sales charges are called no-load funds. See *Load Fund*.

SAME-DAY SUBSTITUTION The purchase and sale on the same day of marginable securities with the same market value thereby avoiding a margin call or a credit to the special miscellaneous account.

SEPARATION THEOREM   The belief that the investment decision is separate from the financing decision. The investment decision involves determining the mix of assets in a given portfolio, while the financing decision involves allocation of investable funds between the risk-free assets and the risky assets. See *Risk-free Asset.*

SERIAL BOND   Bonds that mature at specified stated intervals, imprinted with a sequential serial number at the time of issue.

SETTLEMENT DATE   The date by which a securities transaction must be cleared or settled.

SETTLEMENT PRICE   The final daily market price at which the futures clearinghouse clears all outstanding trades and settles accounts between clearing members. The settlement price and the last transaction price may be different.

SHELF RULE   Permits qualified companies to file a short form registration for securities to be sold over a period of time or off the shelf under favorable conditions.

SHORT AGAINST THE BOX   The act of selling short against a long position in the same stock. Technically, the stock is held in safekeeping by the broker or in the "box". The strategy is used to protect a gain in the long position without having to sell the underlying shares.

SHORT COVERING   The act of purchasing securities to offset securities borrowed for a short sale position.

SHORT HEDGE   A trading strategy that limits the risk of loss in an investment. The short against the box strategy protects an existing holding from decreasing in value via an offsetting rise in the short position.

SHORT INTEREST   The number of shares of a stock that have been sold short but have not yet been covered. Short interest compilations are followed because the short interest represents dormant demand for a stock which may come to life if short sellers must cover their positions due to a marked rise in the stock's price. On the other side of the coin, the higher the short interest in a stock, the more negative investors are about the stock or the company's future earnings potential.

SHORT INTEREST RATIO Technical analysis tool used in evaluating market sentiment. The short interest ratio is calculated by dividing the total sales sold short by the average daily trading volume. Theory based on the assumption that a large short interest position in a stock is a prelude to higher prices for the stock. The rationale for the short interest theory is that the large short position must be covered in the future thereby creating buying pressure and driving the stock price up.

SHORT POSITION The result of having borrowed shares of stock in order to make a short sale.

SHORT SQUEEZE Rapid price rise forcing investors holding short positions to buy securities in order to cut short their losses. This action drives the price up further, squeezing out other short traders substantially increasing their losses.

SPOT MONTH The month that a futures contract becomes deliverable.

SHORT PRICE The actual price quoted for a physical or financial commodity for immediate cash market delivery.

SPREAD The simultaneous sale and purchase of an equivalent option varying in only one condition such as time, maturity or price.

Also, the difference between the price at which a security can be purchased and the price at which it can be sold. See *Asked Price, Bid Price* and *Range*.

STANDARD & POOR'S STOCK PRICE INDEX The S&P 500 index is composed of 400 industrial, 40 financial, 40 public utility and 20 transportation securities. It is a broad-based index designed to measure the value changes of 500 widely owned common stocks. The stocks are weighted to reflect differences in the number of outstanding shares.

STANDARDIZED UNEXPECTED EARNINGS A variable utilized in common stock selection. The standardized unexpected earnings (SUE) is determined by subtracting expected earnings from actual earnings and dividing by the standard error of the regression equation used to estimate the expected earnings.

STOCK The certificates representing ownership in a corporation.

STOCK DIVIDEND The payment of a dividend by a corporation through the issuance of shares instead of cash. Each shareholder would receive a pro rata share of the new issue. Corporations use stock dividends in order to conserve cash for operations.

STOCKHOLDER OF RECORD The shareowner whose name appears on the books of a corporation as of a particular date. The stockholder of record is entitled to receive the dividends and other distributions declared by the Board.

STOCK INDEXES Statistical measurements used in evaluation changes in financial and commodity markets. Stock exchange indexes reflect composite market prices and the number of shares outstanding for corporations comprising the index.

STOCK INDEX FUTURE A futures contract on any of the stock indexes including the NYSE index, S&P 500 or S&P 100, and the Value Line Index.

STOCK POWER An assignment allowing transfer of stock ownership from one party to another party. The stock power gives power of attorney to a third party, usually the transfer agent, to affect the stock ownership transfer between two other parties.

STOP-LIMIT ORDER A buy or sell instruction to the securities broker to make the trade at the specified price or better but only after a specified stop price has been reached or passed. A stop-limit order to sell is effective as soon as there is a sale at the stop price or lower, and then it is executed, if possible, at the limit or higher. Such an offer would read Sell 500 at 13 stop 12 limit. A stop-limit offer avoids the risk associated with stop orders which become market orders when the stop price is attained but runs the risk of not completing the transaction at all if the limit price cannot be obtained.

STOP LOSS An order instruction used by investors to protect existing profits or limit losses. The investor instructs the broker to set a sell price for the specified security at a price below the current market price. If the stock price drops to the stop loss price set by the investor, the order becomes a market order, thereby allowing the investor to close the positioning and preserve profits already earned or limit losses.

STOP ORDER An order instruction to a broker to buy or sell at the market price as soon as the security has traded at a specific price known as the stop price. In a rising market, an investor may use stop orders to protect a gain. As the security's market price rises, the stop order is changed to protect the additional gain. If the stock should then drop to the stop price, the market order is executed, preserving the investor's gain.

STRADDLE Investment strategy combining put and call options on the same investment with the same exercise price and expiration date.

STREET NAME The holding of customer's securities by a brokerage firm in its name. The procedure allows for easier transfer of stock ownership and shares during sale transactions.

STRIKE PRICE   Also called exercise price. The price at which an option or futures contract can be executed according to the terms of the contract. For example, a call option to purchase Chrysler at $12 a share through the September expiration date has a striking price of $12 a share. If Chrysler is currently trading at $14 1/2 a share and the investor believes that will probably be the top until the expiration date of the call, he would execute the call option at $12 a share and earn $2 a share ($14 1/2-$12) less commissions.

STRONG FORM   That part of the efficient market theory which states that prices reflect all information, public and private.

SUBORDINATED DEBENTURE   A debenture bond with lower repayment rights than other senior contractual debt. Since the risk is higher, subordinated debentures tend to carry higher interest rates or have a higher discount in the secondary market.

SUBSCRIPTION PRICE   The price at which existing shareholders can purchase additional shares in accordance with a rights offering or subscription right.

SWITCH   A commodity futures trading program that offsets a position in one delivery month and simultaneously opens a similar position in another delivery month for the same commodity.

SYSTEMATIC RISK   The risk attributable to factors affecting all investments. Also called market risk or non-diversifiable risk.

T

10K, 10Q   The annual and quarterly reports required by the SEC which must be filed by corporations traded on organized exchanges and the over-the-counter NASDAQ market. These reports contain a wealth of information for the investor. They are considered "must" reading for informed investors. Although annual reports contain the basics of financial reporting, the 10k features more in-depth information on the company's products, market segments, competitors, plant facilities, customers, management, and legal proceedings. The 10q quarterly reports issued since the last annual report will present more recent events affecting company earnings and operations. It provides more detailed information on quarterly results, earnings and expense classifications, and significant events than the quarterly earnings release or shareholders report.

TEAR SHEET   Information sheet on individual companies published by Standard & Poor's. The name derives from the fact that brokers tear the sheets out of the ring binders and send them to their customers.

TECHNICAL ANALYSIS   An investment technique which analyzes market and stock price and volume trends with the purpose of establishing buy and sell strategies. Technical analysts use charting and/or computer analysis programs to isolate price and volume movements which are believed to signal market and individual stock price movements. Most technical analysis is short-to-intermediate-term.

TECHNICAL SIGN   A price movement which technical analysis can identify as an important move or shift of direction in terms of its chart pattern.

TENDER   To surrender shares in response to a tender offer by a corporation or others to purchase the shares at a specified price within a specified period of time.

TENDER OFFER   A bid to buy any or all of a corporation's outstanding shares, usually at a premium to current market value, by an individual, group or corporation seeking control. The takeover tender offer must be filed with the SEC prior to public announcement.

TERM BOND   A corporate or municipal bond with a single long-term maturity date.

THEORETICAL VALUE OF A WARRANT   Formula value for a warrant which determines its intrinsic value. Since the theoretical value does not take into account market factors the warrant will usually trade above the intrinsic value.

TICK   Price movement of a stock originally derived from ticker tapes. An uptick is a upward price movement, a downtick is a downward price movement.

TICKER SYMBOL   The letters that are used to designate a particular stock for trading transactions. Trades are reported on the consolidated tape and on quote machines by the company's ticker symbol. For example, the ticker symbol for USX corporation is X.

TIGHT MARKET   A market for a specific security, or the market in general that is characterized by very competitive, active trading. The spread between bid and ask price is very narrow in tight markets.

TIME VALUE   A factor used in determining the option premium for a particular option. It is also considered the difference between the premium of an option and its intrinsic value. For instance, an option with a premium of $40 and an intrinsic value of $35 would have a time value of $5.

TOEHOLD PURCHASE   The purchase of less than 5% of the outstanding stock of a company which is a target acquisition. After 5% has been acquired, notification to the SEC, the appropriate stock exchange, and the target company is made.

TOMBSTONE   The newspaper advertisement placed by underwriters of public distributions of securities. It is not an offer to sell or a solicitation of an offer to buy. It provides minimal information about the offer and refers readers to the prospectus for details of the issue. Many underwriters use tombstones to advertise their role in mergers, private placements, and acquisitions. See *Prospectus*.

TOP Stock or market high point which will be followed by a consolidation and/or decline in stock prices.

TOPS AND BOTTOMS Various chart patterns reflecting stock and market movements.

TOP-DOWN INVESTING Investment strategy concentrating on looking at the economic scenario first before narrowing down investment options in specific industries and companies. See *Bottom-up Investing*.

TOTAL RETURN The calculation of yield which takes into account both dividend and interest income plus appreciation of the investment principal. Total return for bonds is yield to maturity. For stocks, estimated return based on the security's price/earnings ratio is added to the dividend yield.

TOTAL VOLUME The total number of shares traded in a day whether on the stock exchanges or in the over-the-counter markets. For instance, a stock traded on the New York Exchange could also be traded on a regional exchange and in the over-the-counter market. The total volume for that stock would be the aggregate volume from all trades of the stock no matter where traded.

TWO-DOLLAR BROKER Member of the New York Stock Exchange who executes orders on the floor of the exchange for other members having more volume than they can handle at a particular time. They also execute orders for firms who do not have their own exchange member on the floor. Originally called $2 brokers because their round lot commission was fixed at $2. Now commissions between $2 brokers and commission brokers are negotiated. Also called independent broker.

U

UNCOVERED OPTION   Also called naked option. An uncovered option is any option that the buyer or seller does not have covered with an underlying security position.

UNDERLYING SECURITY   In regard to stock options, the underlying security is the security which must be delivered when an option is exercised. Index options are settled in cash.

An underlying security is also the common stock that must be delivered by the corporation in exchange for subscription rights, subscription warrants, convertible bonds or convertible preferred stock.

V

VARIABLE ANNUITY   A life insurance investment contract whose value is determined by the changing value of the underlying portfolio of debt and equity securities. Variable annuities may be purchased with a lump sum payment or a number of installment payments. The payout may be a stream of periodic payments which vary with the market value of the portfolio or a fixed payment amount with possible add-ons based on the increased market value of the underlying portfolio. See *Annuity* and *Fixed Annuity*.

VARIABLE RATE SECURITY   Any security with provisions for recalculating the rate of return based on specific indexes. The interest rate is recalculated at specific intervals based on changes in the underlying index or indexes.

VERTICAL LINE CHARTING   Technical analysis chart technique that utilizes a vertical line to indicate the high and low for the period and a horizontal line to indicate the closing price. The chart over a period of time' shows the trend of the security or market index being charted.

VERTICAL SPREAD An option trading strategy with the investor establishing both long and short option positions in the same underlying security with the same expiration dates but with different strike prices.

V FORMATION A stock or commodity chart pattern that outlines a "V". The trend is considered bullish if the "V" is upright and bearish if the "V" is inverted.

VOLATILE A stock, bond, commodity or market that is susceptible to rapid price variations. The measure of a stock's volatility to the market in general is called its beta. A beta greater than 1 indicates more volatility than others for a variety of reasons. The stock's industry may be very volatile. For instance, gold mining stocks and toy company stocks have histories of volatile price movements. See *Data*.

W

WITH OR WITHOUT With or without or "W.O.W." orders are limited orders which are executed either on the quotation or on the round lot sale, whichever is effective. If the offer is filled on the quotation, the odd-lot differential is subtracted from the bid in the case of a sale or added to the offer in case of a purchase. If the order is filled on the basis or a round lot sale, the rules for limited order apply.

WORKING CAPITAL The excess of current assets over current liabilities. Working capital is composed of the firm's cash, marketable securities, accounts receivable, and inventory.

WORKING CONTROL The condition existing when a shareholder owning less that 51% of the shares or having less than 51% of the voting interest controls corporate policy and actions.

WRAPAROUND ANNUITY An insurance company contract that provides tax sheltered dividends, interest, and capital appreciation while allowing the subscriber some choice of fund investment.

WRITE OUT Transaction made by a specialist and within exchange guidelines involving the specialist's own securities inventory. A write out would entail a trade between the broker and the specialist followed by a separate trade with the client. Normal broker's commissions are charged for write out trades.

WRITER An investor that sells an option contract and earns premium income. The writer is obligated to deliver the security in the case of a call option or to purchase the security in the case of a put option. Options may be written covered (with the underlying security position) or naked (without the underlying security position).

X

XD Abbreviation used to designate ex-dividend.

XR Abbreviation used to designate stocks trading ex-rights.

Y

YANKEE BOND An international bond issued by foreign banks and corporations but trading in U.S. dollars and registered for sale in the United States. Yankee bonds may have favorable tax status in certain countries.

YIELD An investor's percentage return on security investments. For stock, it is the return earned from common stock or preferred dividends. For bonds, it is the coupon rate of return divided by the bond purchase price.

YIELD ADVANTAGE The difference in the yield that can be earned investing in a convertible security versus the yield offered on the underlying common stock security. For example, if a convertible preferred security currently yields 8% and the common stock current yield is 4 1/2%, the yield advantage for the convertible preferred stocks 3 1/2%.

YIELD CURVE   A graph illustrating the relationship of interest rate yields to time for various fixed-income securities of the same class. If short-term rates are lower, the yield curve is positive. If short-term rates are higher , the yield curve is negative. Usually, yield curves are positive since investors want to be compensated for the additional risk associated with investing for longer periods of time. Yield curves can help in the analysis of interest rate trends.

YIELD EQUIVALENCE   The interest rate which provides the same return for both tax-exempt and taxable securities.

YIELD SPREADS   The relationships between bond yields and the particular features on various bonds such as quality, callability, and taxes. Also, the difference between stock dividend yield and the current yield on bonds.

Index

A

accountant's or auditor's option   93
accrued interest   94
accumulated dividend   94
accumulation area   94
acid-test ratio   94
active market   94
Additional Purchases   69–76
Adjusted Point Score   38
advance-decline line   95
after tax basis   95
against the box   95
all or none   95
American Depository Receipts (ADR)   21, 93
American Stock Exchange   11, 16, 19
analyst   96
annual basis   96
annual report   96
annuity   96
arbitrage   96
ascending tops   97
asked price   97
asset allocation   97
asset management account   97
asset play   97
at the close   97
at the market   97
at the money   97
at the opening   97
authorized shares   98
average down, average up   98

Awarding Points   26–33
away from the market   98

B

back-end load   98
balanced mutual fund   98
bankruptcy   98
Barron's or Investor's Daily   22
basis   99
basis point   99
basis price   99
bear   99
bear market   99
bearer security   99
bellwether   99
beta   100
bid price   100
blind pool   100
block trading   100
blue chip   100
bond   100
bond rating   101
bond ratio   101
book value   101
bottom   101
bottom up investing   102
break   102
breakout   102
brokerage houses   2
bull   102
bullmarket   102

C

call option   102
calls   102
capitalization ratio   103
cash equivalent   103
cash flow   103
cash ratio   103

charting   103
circuit breaker   103
Class A   16
Class B   16
close   103
closed-end fund   104
commodity future   104
common stock   104
common stock equivalent   104
common stock ratio   104
contingent liabilities   104
Continuing the Illustration   59–69
currency futures   105
current ratio   105
current yield   105
customer's loan consent   105
cyclical   105

D

daily trade limit   105
date of record   105
day order   106
debenture   106
debt-to-equity ratio   106
deep discount bond   106
defensive securities or industries   106
delayed opening   106
depository receipt   106
descending tops   106
differential   106
dilution   107
dip   107
disclosure   107
discount broker   107
discretionary account   107
diversification   33, 107
dividend   108
dividend payout ratio   108
Dividend Record   53
dividend reinvestment plan   108

Dow Chemical (DOW)   11
Dow Industrial Average   1
Ducommon, Inc. (DCO)   11

E

earnings per share (EPS)   8, 108
economic indicators   108
effective rate   108
efficient market   109
equity   109
equivalent bond yield   109
Erlich, Harold   3
ex-dividend   109

F

figuring percentages   83
fill   109
fill or kill   109
filter rule   109
Final Selection, The   33–35
financial future   109
Financial Situation, The   13–14
first call date   110
fiscal year   110
fixed annuity   110
fixed-charged coverage   110
fixed-income security   110
flag   110
flash   110
flat bond   110
flat market   111
float   111
floor broker   111
floor trader   111
forced conversion   111
formula investing   111
forward contract   111
fourth market   111
fractional discretion order   112

Freddie Mac   112
free credit balance   112
front-end load   112
full-service broker   35, 112
fully diluted earnings per share   112
fundamental analysis   113
futures contract   113
futures exchange   113

G

golden parachute   114
good delivery   114
Good Till Cancelled (GTC)   56
good-till-cancelled order   114
grantor   114
greenmail   114
gross spread   115
growth fund   115
growth investments   115
guaranteed bond   115

H

head and shoulders   115
hedging   115
high flyer   116
high-grade bond   116
high-premium convertible bond   116
high-tech stock   116
historic trading ranges   116
historic yield   116
holder of record   117

I

Illustration of the System   38–39
imbalance of orders   117
immediate payment annuity   117
in the money   119
incovered option   142

Increased Earnings   7–11
   "But" No. 1   8–9
   "But" No. 2   9–11
individual retirement account (IRA)   117
Industries   79–81
Industry Code 48   38
initial margin   118
Initial Public Offering (IPO)   118
initial stops   69
inside information   118
inside market   118
insider   118
institutional broker   118
instiutional investor   119
insured account   119
intercommodity spread   119
interdelivery spread   119

L

liquidity   119
listed option   119
listed stock   120
load fund   120
loaned flat   120
locked market   120

M

M1   120
M2   120
M3 M2   121
maintenance margin   121
major securities firms   1
managed account   121
margin   121
margin agreement   121
margin call   121
mark to the market   122
market breadth   121
market if touched order (MIT)   122

market order   122
market price   122
market timing   122
market maker   122
market tone   122
Mayday   123
minus tick   123
Myth No. 1   5
Myth No. 2   5

N

NASDAQ Trading System symbols   16
New York Stock Exchange   11, 16, 19
no-par stock   123
nonrefundable   123
Not Held (NH)   123
Note Rated (NR)   123

O

odd lot   124
odd-ball theories   123
original issue discount bond   124
out of the money   124
over-the-counter (OTC)   19, 56, 124
Overall Quality, The   14

P

P/E as % of WAG   30
par value   124
parity   124
participating preferred stock   125
passed dividend   125
paydown   125
payment date   125
payout ratio   125
pennant   125
penny stocks   126
performance fund   126

performance stock   126
periodic payment plan   126
perpendicular spread   126
Picking the "Semi-Finalists"   16–26
pink sheet stocks   126
plan completion insurance   127
premium   127
premium income   127
price continuity   127
price to earnings ratio   4, 12, 13, 27, 127
Price/Earnings Ratio, The   11–12
program trading   127
prospectus   128
proxy   128
Purchase Only A+ Rated Stocks   46
put option   128

Q

qualitative analysis   128
quantitative analysis   128
quick ratio   129
quiet period   129
quote   129

R

range   129
rating   129
ratio analysis   129
realized yield   130
recorded date   130
red herring   130
redemption   130
registered security   130
rehypothecation   130
reinvestment rate risk   130
Relation of P/E to Growth   12–13
relative strength   131
residual security   131
resistance level   131

restricted account   131
retirement   131
reversal   131
reverse split   131
reward-to-variability ratio   132
reward-to-volatility ratio   132
right   132
risk   132
risk premium   133
risk-averse investor   132
risk-free asset   133
risk-free rate of return   133
risk-sensitive   133
round lot   133
round turn   133

S

S & P Rating   30
sales charge   133
same-day substitution   133
self-discipline   78
sell a stock, reasons to   58
sell stop   56
   lower the stop   57
separation theorem   134
serial bond   134
settlement date   134
settlement price   134
shelf rule   134
short against the box   134
short covering   134
short hedge   134
short interest   134
short interest ratio   135
short position   135
short price   135
short squeeze   135
spot month   135
spread   135
Standard & Poor's Corporation   15

Standard & Poor's Corporation Security Owner's Stock Guide
    14, 15, 16, 85
  %Div. Yield   20, 30
  Book Value   22
  Capitalization   21, 22
  Cash Div. Ea. Yr. Since   20
  Com. Rank. & Pfd. Rating   19
  Dividends   20
  Earnings   21
  Earnings Per Share   22
  Equity Per Share   22
  Financial Position   20, 22
  Index   16
  Inst. Hold.   19
  Interim Earnings   21, 23
  Last Sale of Bid   20
  Month's Sales in 100's   19
  Name of Issue   19, 21
  Net Asset Value   22
  P/E Ratio   20, 22
  Par Value   19
  Price Range   19
  Principal Business   19
  S & P ratings   14, 30
  Ticker Symbol   16
Standard & Poor's Stock Price Index   136
standardized unexpected earnings   136
stock   136
stock dividend   136
stock index future   136
stock indexes   136
stock power   136
Stock Purchases   35–37
Stock Sheet   49–51
stockholder of record   136
stop loss   137
stop order   137
stop-limit order   137
straddle   137
street name   137
strike price   138

strong form   138
subordinated debenture   138
subscription price   138
Summary Sheet   51–53
switch   138
system advantages   77
systematic risk   138

T

10K, 10Q   138
tear sheet   139
technical analysis   139
technical sign   139
tender   139
tender offer   139
term bond   140
theoretical value of a warrant   140
tick   140
ticker symbol   140
tight market   140
time value   140
toehold purchase   140
tombstone   140
top   141
top-down investing   141
tops and bottoms   141
total return   141
total volume   141
two-dollar broker   141

U

uncovered optoin   142
underlying security   142
Use a Combination System   47

V

V formation   143
variable annuity   142
variable rate security   142

vertical line charting   142
vertical spread   143
volatile   143

W

Weekly Price Chart   53–59, 60
weighted average growth   9, 13, 26
with or without   143
working capital   143
working control   143
wraparound annuity   144
write out   144
writer   144

X

XD   144
XR   144

Y

Yankee bond   144
yield   144
yield advantage   144
yield curve   145
yield equivalence   145
yield spreads   145